Who Killed the Berkeley School?

WHO KILLED
THE BERKELEY SCHOOL?
STRUGGLES OVER
RADICAL CRIMINOLOGY

Herman & Julia
Schwendinger

Thought | Crimes
2014

Who Killed the Berkeley School? Struggles Over Radical Criminology

First published in 2014 by
Thought | Crimes

an imprint of punctum books * brooklyn, ny

Ⓟ http://punctumbooks.com

& design/layout: pj lilley

and the full book is available for download via our
Open Monograph Press website (a Public Knowledge Project) at:

http://www.thoughtcrimespress.org

a project of the Critical Criminology Working Group,
(publishers of the Open Access Journal: *Radical Criminology*):
http://journal.radicalcriminology.org
Contact: Jeff Shantz (Editor), Dept. of Criminology, KPU
12666 72 Ave. Surrey, BC V3W 2M8

ISBN-13: 978-0615990934
ISBN-10: 0615990932

To Julia
(1926–2013)

Contents

Foreword
"Radical Criminology Lives"

The assault on the Berkeley School of Criminology (at the University of California-Berkeley), a hub of radical organizing, theorizing, and action, is one of the likely forgotten or overlooked (or never known) salvos of Ronald Reagan's frontal assaults on dissent and resistance (particularly in domestic terms). Launched in the 1960s and carried out extensively between 1973 and 1976, the campaign against the Berkeley School radicals would see final victory in 1977.

In this engaging and pointed book Julia and Herman Schwendinger, two key participants in the Berkeley School (and two who were penalized for their committed involvement in the school and broader community struggles against exploitation and oppression), provide important insights and open, honest, unflinching assessment of these battles. They provide crucial lessons for contemporary organizers and activists in the academy, and beyond, and reinforce the great need for radicalism within disciplines like criminology that are supposed to identify, analyze, and end practices (and causes) of social harm. And speak out against the role of power holders in generating and reproducing social harm.

Like the better known attack on the air traffic controllers union only three years later, the breaking of the Berkeley School would decimate an infrastructure of resistance to neoliberal capitalism (and ideologies expressed in New Right criminology in this case) in its early stages as well as sending a message to possible allies that they should watch their step (lest they endure a similar fate). It also, like the air traffic controllers struggle, tested the resolve of neoliberalism's potential opponents—and the willingness of "soft supporters" or liberal forces to act on behalf of those caught in the crosshairs. In both cases the broad oppositional forces, and particularly potential allies and soft supporters, were found fatally wanting. And the emergent forces of neoliberal reaction (and New Right ideology) gained important victories and developed new confidence to push on.

The Berkeley School radicals identified the real sources of social harm in society—state, military, and corporate actions. They also insisted on calling these harms by their proper name—crimes. They openly identified the wars against Indigenous peoples across Turtle Island as what they were—campaigns of genocide. The Vietnam assault was recognized not as unfortunate war, geopolitical event, or American crisis (or tragedy) but, unflinchingly, as a criminal endeavor undertaken by the US state. The Schwendingers lay out the captive place of the university in the military-industrial-complex, detailing the depth and breadth of corporate influence and control.

Most of all, the Berkeley School radicals, perhaps more than any academic criminologists before or since, bridged the false gap between community resistance and academic labors. They immersed themselves in struggles, not apart from or in conflict with their roles as researchers, learners, and/or knowledge producers—but as a direct outcome of those pursuits. For this they were targeted by politicians and administrators. Punished as community members and activists, reprimanded and fired as intellectual workers.

The Berkeley School stands as a model toward which contemporary critical (even better, radical) criminology might strive. The account by the Schwendingers offers both a guide to organizing in the present and a caution about steps to avoid and the lessons learned through real struggle.

This compelling work reminds us of a criminology not of the classroom but of the communities and workplaces. It reminds us of a criminology of active resistance. It is a criminology rooted in real world responses to ongoing concerns about social harms in communities most subjected to those harms. This is a criminology that is neither utopian nor ideological because it actually identifies and names the social structures and relations that cause social harms and which prevent them from being addressed. And it openly confronts and challenges those exploitative and oppressive structures and relations (rather than accepting them merely as objects of study).

This is also a proposal and an invitation. Not only to radicals but to those who claim to be critical in good times but become "pragmatists" or "realists" when it affects them personally (with apologies to Phil Ochs). Criminologists in pursuing social justice will, eventually (and must) offend university administrators, criminal justice officials, law enforcement agents, and politicians. We should not apologize for this nor should we hide our analysis away in the comfort of lecture halls, seminars, or conferences.

Compromise has become a signal word of the neoliberal period (like the "consensus" of an earlier epoch). Yet compromise tends to overlook the imbalance of forces—of resources, of power, and of harm. It offers a profoundly unjust equalization of (unequal) responsibility and obscures the fact that certain groups (classes, strata) bear the brunt of harms inflicted one-sidedly by another group (class, stratum). This compromise almost always ends up satisfying (and justifying) power holders.

The current period of New Right hegemony (in government, media, and the academy) and the decades long promotion of law and order ideology as public policy, requires, finally, an active, organized opposition from criminology that is based not only in (ineffectual) critique but political mobilization in solidarity and community with those who have been subjected to the right wing onslaught.

This is a crucial history, a significant example of struggle. It is relevant for anyone interested in the development of neoliberal capitalism and austerity governance. It is required reading for anyone concerned with building infrastructures of resistance in the current context and, particularly, linking the struggles of campus and community in a way that might challenge dominant structures and relations of ruling and forge and maintain connections of solidarity and active resistance.

The assault on the Berkeley School radicals was nothing short of, as the Schwendingers state it, "the repression of a struggle for justice." And it had lasting impacts, both on social struggles and on the development of criminology (which shadowed the Reaganomics of the 1980s with New Right ideology and 'broken windows' class violence).

More than a work of criminology, this is a vibrant and honest telling of overlooked histories of radical struggle (and the perhaps surprising, for current audiences, part played by criminology in solidarity with movements of the poor and oppressed). It fills in missing pieces in the history of the peoples' liberation movements of the late twentieth century.

As the Schwendingers note, it is impossible to understand radicalism (or criminology) without recognizing social context. In particular it is necessary to understand particular contexts of social struggle, social movement, and change. The interface of social and political movements, and the place of criminologists within these (radical or otherwise), is important.

In the context of Occupy mobilizations and mass repression in various sites (including extensive violence by police at the University of California-Berkeley itself) this is essential reading for anyone seeking a deeper understanding of repression and resistance. The Schwendingers' recount tactics, such as early manifestations of kettling, that are perhaps too often viewed as recent manifestations of neoliberal policing practice.

Readers might also note the use of demonizing language to discredit all forms of resistance. The phantom communist of the 1960s and 1970s has been morphed by state capital into the phantom terrorist of today. In each case the specter is used by governments to justify growing uses of repressive violence, illegal state surveillance, and violations of civil and human rights.

As critical thinking in the academy is sacrificed to concerns of the labor market or "relevance" (for whom?) and technocratism, managerialism, and expediency drive "curriculum," over scholarship broadly conceived, this story has much to tell us. This is a living and vital document of a vital (and still living) movement and project. It should be read, reread, studied and, most importantly, built upon in practice.

In the era of neoliberal austerity and "law and order" hegemony it is as pressing as ever that criminologists demystify traditional rationales for exploitation and oppression. Indeed, criminologists must address the very nature and aims of criminology in this period of surveillance and repression. As the Schwendingers ask, how can conscientious criminology students and faculty, whose very subject of study is crime, remain quiet in the face of state and capitalist atrocities? The answer remains, now as then—we can't.

Jeff Shantz

Kwantlen Polytechnic University

Surrey (Newton), British Columbia

Introduction
Déjà Vu

During the 1960s and 1970s, The School of Criminology at the University of California Berkeley (UCB) had more than 30 full-time or part-time faculty members teaching upper-division and graduate courses in criminalistics and criminology. The School was the leading American institution devoted to criminology. Nevertheless, it was abolished in 1977 by California's Governor, Ronald Reagan, and the UCB Chancellor, Alfred Bowker.

Bowker in later years defended himself by saying the School had become "politicized"—implying that it no longer fulfilled its academic responsibilities. But his allegation was false. The School was closed because a group of 30 students and 4 faculty members had fought against the brutal suppression of political dissent as well as the racist and sexist law-enforcement policies prevailing throughout the country. These members also opposed the crimes being committed by the United States in the Vietnam War. They enhanced the academic status of the School among criminologists in the United States and Europe. They did not reduce that status.

Members of this group became "usual suspects" because they joined the thousands in the San Francisco Bay Area who had protested the crimes inflicted by the U.S. government during the War. In fact, the events leading to the School's closing began when they publically expressed their outrage over the brutal suppression of "Stop the Draft Week" demonstrations in 1967.

These members were attacked by university officials even though they epitomized the highest ideals of their profession. They had opposed the devastation of Vietnam, Cambodia and Laos because the U.S. government was creating landscapes overflowing with land mines, toxic chemicals, mutilated people, and corpses. The U.S. Air Force had strafed *everything that moved* including farm animals, children, old people, women and men.

Simultaneously, when political dissent erupted through the United States after Cambodia was invaded, civil liberties were lawlessly assaulted by the CIA, FBI, state, and local police. In Berkeley, Reagan sent an armed convoy of National Guardsmen to control this dissent.

Further examples starting with genocidal wars against Native Americans and the 1798 Alien and Sedition Acts demonstrate that the U.S. government has never been the entity idealized by public school civics lessons. Like Janus, the Roman God of gateways and exits, the Statue of Liberty, the gateway to the U.S. signals a vista of democratic spirits and American dreams. But that vista is periodically eclipsed by the suppression of civil liberties and human rights.

1 | Gilbert Geis' Autopsy

G ilbert Geis, an academic criminologist, conducted a fantastical autopsy twenty years after the School of Criminology was assassinated. Geis accomplished this amazing feat even though he wasn't at the scene of the crime and the corpse was decomposed, so he could not put it under his knife. Nonetheless, he was able to scrutinize recollections and documents by onlookers and perps who were at the scene. With such so-called "indisputable facts" he cobbled an explanation of why the School was killed and who did it in.

In a section entitled, *Postmortem Lividity,* Geis stated, "the School of Criminology did not fade away quietly, though the Sindler report[1] virtually dictated its demise. Torrents of words were written into the record between the end of 1973 and July 15, 1976, when the guillotine finally dropped by formal approval of the regents." However, in Geis' view, none of the perps including UCB Chancellor Bowker and Prof. Alan Sindler actually committed the crime intentionally. They may have committed *schoolslaughter* but not murder in the first de-

---

1 An in-house committee, appointed by UCB administration and chaired by Alan Sindler, wrote the report.

3

gree, that is, not with malice aforethought. They acted impetuously—only committing the crime after being provoked by the radicals.[2]

To back this verdict, Geis rounded up the usual suspects.[3] The radicals, he declares, were in no small part responsible because of their unwillingness to compromise. Instead, they stubbornly continued to make "themselves highly visible and, from the viewpoint of the university administration, embarrassingly unpopular not only with it, but also with the local law enforcement establishment." "They also offended California's Governor, Ronald Reagan and Edwin Meese III, then the governor's legal affairs secretary, on the school's advisory council." Consequently, in Geis' opinion, the radicals' stubborn willfulness should also be blamed. These emotionally charged individuals wanted to become martyrs. They were unwilling to stay in the closet and discontinue their "highly publicized acts of political protest."

Geis took pains to let everyone know his coroner's report was impartial and scolded the University authorities as well. He accused them of being "insensitive" and

---

2 Gilbert Geis, "The Limits of Academic Tolerance: The Discontinuance of the School of Criminology at Berkeley." In *Punishment and Social Control: Essays in Honor of Sheldon L. Messinger.* (Eds. Thomas G. Blomberg and Stanley Cohen. New York: Aldine de Gruyter, 1995 pp. 280–281).

3 The phrase, "usual suspects" is borrowed from a remark by Claude Raines in the movie, Casablanca. In that film, Captain Louis Renault (played by Claude Raines) witnesses Rick Blaine (Humphrey Bogart) shoot the German officer, Major Strasser (Conrad Veidt). Upon hearing the shot, gendarmes rush to the scene of the crime; but Captain Renault merely exclaims, "Major Strasser's been shot." He pauses as he looks at Rick and then casually turns to the gendarmes, saying, "Round up the usual suspects!" The gendarmes obediently drive away and Rick gets away with murder.

"mulish" and, consequently, contributing to a mutual failure at communication and compromise.

What we had, then, was a jousting match, often tasteless, at least if dignity is the judgment criterion characterized on one side by partisan beliefs and, on the other, by rather implacable insensitivity. There was no question where the ultimate power lay, though those who lost out seemed astonishingly unaware of what social class and governmental forces dominated political developments even though these forces used their power effectively.[4]

How should we, as two of these radicals, respond to Geis? Perhaps we should use stronger language to counter his claim that the radicals were indifferent to the School's closing or that they wanted martyrdom. But, with the passage of time, we will simply observe that he trivialized the forces, motives, and actions leading to the closing of the School. His interpretation reduced the repression of a struggle for justice and an end to the slaughter in Vietnam to a "jousting match." His use of psychological causes (like "willfulness" and "mulishness") is preposterous. Further, since the radicals—certainly not the administrative authorities—were harmed, his theory blames the victims of the crime.

To warrant his reference to radical "willfulness," Geis regurgitated Bowker and Sindler's cover stories. Discussing the nature of the conflict between the administration and radicals, he says the radicals refused to recognize criticisms aimed at the School. He validates this false assertion with phony circumstantial evidence. He claims that the quality of the Criminology faculty was questionable. The integrity of their curriculum was dubious. The academic and public services performed by

---

4 Ibid.

the School needed "shoring up." The radicals, he added, also needed to come to agreement with the administration about "tolerable and intolerable" behavior in classrooms although, *of course*, by his own admission, agreement on this option was never in the cards because each side "mulishly refused to grant legitimacy to the concerns of the other but rather took refuge behind its own rhetoric ..."

Geis misinforms readers when he calls Bowker's and the Sindler Committee's reservations about the school "indisputable facts." His claim had no basis in reality. The school was purported to oppose "professional" goals and resist servicing the law enforcement establishment. Yet the School's program produced qualified forensic experts. Its faculty had engaged in experiments expanding their field of knowledge. It was consulted by prosecutors, defense attorneys, and police. In addition, other faculty members, such as Jerome Skolnick, serviced crime commissions. Another member, Bernard Diamond, repeatedly provided expert testimony for defense attorneys. Richard Korn and David Vogel conducted projects aimed at educating judges. The School sponsored a pioneering prisoner education program at San Quentin. An LEAA funded Master's degree program serviced police officers drawn from various parts of the United States. Tony Platt helped criminal-justice reform groups formulate model legislation while Paul Takagi served as a consultant for criminal justice agencies. Even Herman Schwendinger contributed to criminal justice programs although he usually focused on theoretical approaches to crime causation rather than control.[5]

---

5 In fact, he had received a research grant larger than any other member on the faculty had received—over a half million dollars— to pursue his investigation of illegal markets. To obtain the grant, he was required to select someone who could monitor his

Schwendinger taught a seminar in a Master's program designed for police officers and made repeated visits to Pacifica, south of San Francisco, in response to a request from the officer handling juvenile crime. With Takagi, Schwendinger obtained National Institute of Health and Welfare funds for organizing a conference on delinquency control. He had also testified in person before the Congressional Subcommittee on Crime and the Judiciary about federal funding for delinquency programs.. He never divorced himself from these kinds of activities.

Furthermore, most of the research conducted by the School's doctoral students focused on law enforcement policies and penal institutions. The research represented an array of professionally oriented topics such as the creation of drug policies to the control of prison populations. Other topics include the impact of drug control policies on communities of urban drug users, the formation of police in the 18th century, the Benthamite movement for legal reform in England, the economic foundations of classical criminology, the rise of convict labor in America, the emergence of prostitution in a Western frontier community, the relations between the police and women's suffrage movements, and grassroots organizations devoted to reforming the ways that medical and law enforcement agencies treated rape victims.

Geis insists that the radicals were not reasonable because they were shortsighted, highly emotional utopians. To prove this point, he sprinkles his article by citing the radicals themselves. He quotes Tony Platt's writings about the "theoretical weaknesses of radical criminolo-

---

expenditures because the grant was awarded shortly before he received his doctoral degree at UCLA. Joseph Lohman, the Dean of the School of Criminology offered to become a co-sponsor to meet this requirement.

gy" that indicated it suffered from short-term activism and idealist expectations about the impact of social protest.[6] Geis also cited a personal communication where "Platt said that, if he had it to do over, he would seek to form better strategic alliances to try to guarantee the school's survival." Yet Platt, whose courage was indisputable, added that he has had no regrets even though he with other radicals "were optimistic in the way that utopians often are."[7]

Geis quotes liberal authorities on the Sixties to discredit the tactics supported by radicals at the School. Although Todd Gitlin's work is an inadequate framework for understanding the *breadth* and *diversity* of protest activity in the Sixties,[8] Geis says Gitlin's "sophisticated retrospective" provides further support for condemning the radicals. Gitlin had observed that the early idealism of Berkeley's Students for a Democratic Society (SDS) came apart because of "its commitment to an impossible

---

6 Geis quotes Platt's letter: "Radical criminology in its earliest days tended toward ultraleftism, romanticism, and a messianic utopianism." In Anthony M. Platt, personal communication to Geis, October 30, 1993.

7 Geis quotes Platt who said, "Obviously, from the way things turned out, we were misguided; otherwise we wouldn't have done it." However, this statement should not be taken at face value because Geis does not provide its context. Finally, there were differences among the radicals that sharply contradict Geis' interpretations and stereotypes.

8 Andrew Hunt points this out "When Did the Sixties Happen? Searching for New Directions." *Journal of Social History*. Also, criticism of Gitlin's thesis indicates other reasons for the SDS' demise; for instance, see Nancy Zaroulis and Gerald Sullivan, *Who Spoke Up? American Protest Against the War in Vietnam 1963-1975*. Finally, Gitlin, in our opinion, ignores significant differences within the SDS on lower organizational levels, especially regarding 'violent' and 'nonviolent' tactics.

revolution" and because of its "passionate hairsplitting, irresponsible leaders, desperado strategy, insupportable tactics." Geis obviously believes the Criminology radicals were no different.[9]

Finally, Stan Cohen is brought into play as an authority on how the radicals behaved or what they believed.[10] Geis claims that Cohen offers us an informative "lesson on how the emergent women's movement, with its focus on rape, trashed the radical movement's romantic portrait of criminals as politically oppressed, deserving of sympathy." Even though radicals in Criminology *never* romanticized rapists and most shared similar ideas and reformist agendas, Geis concludes:

> . . . critical scholarship has well exposed the problems of this original agenda, but the very effectiveness of the demystification job is a little embarrassing. One has to distance oneself from those original ideas and reforms: dismiss one's enthusiastic support for them as matters of false consciousness or perhaps a product of overenthusiastic youthful exuberance.

Geis says, "Cohen warns against radical impossibilism, which asserts that all reforms are doomed. There is evidence enough that the upheavals of the Sixties produced meaningful change. But how does it all add up?" Obvi-

---

9 Geis, op. cit. p. 987.

10 According to Geis, Cohen regards his own works during the Sixties and Seventies as "brash, simplistic, and tendentious." This may be true but whether they were radical is another matter – we found no writings validating that status. When he was a Visiting Professor (from England) at the School, his professional associations were apolitical and he wasn't involved in any radical project or protest movement.

ously, if Geis' account is to be believed, it all adds up to a tragedy of displaced passions and a valiant but impossible attempt to scale the heavens.

2 | How Does It *Really* Add Up?

A lthough the School of Criminology's assassination occurred over 35 years ago and the radicals were framed for the murder, the contract for the kill was actually fulfilled by government and university officials. The perps even included faculty whose cowardice or commitment to "friendly fascism"[1] was bred by decades of McCarthyism and the Cold War.

The officials—Ronald Reagan, Richard Nixon, Spiro Agnew and J. Edgar Hoover—provided ordnance for the on-campus assassination team. Their arsenal of demagogic injunctions, covert surveillance, police repression and budget cuts rallied the team's supporters, neutralized its opposition and extorted cooperation and silence from the faculty at large. Reagan, who had been an informer for the House Un-American Activities Committee long before he became Governor in 1966, had promised to cut the budget and clean up "the mess in Berkeley." To monitor the School of Criminology, he appointed his "trou-

---

1 The phrase, "friendly fascism," is borrowed from Bertram Gross, *Friendly Fascism: The New Face of Power in America.* (New York: Evans and Co. 1980), where he suggests that, unlike Germany, police state developments will appear in stages rather than emerge full-blown in a short period of time.

bleshooter," Edwin Meese III, to its Advisory Council.[2] He also appointed people like Max Rafferty, the notoriously right-wing State Superintendent of Public Instruction, as University of California Regents. The Regents in turn stepped-up their opposition to campus civil liberties and anti-war movements.

The 24 Regents and their powerful associates owned and operated the State of California. None of the Regents except Max Rafferty, whose worthlessness as a professional had become legendary, were educators by profession. Even H.R. Haldeman of Watergate fame was a Regent before he resigned to join the Nixon administration. When their stock portfolios were disclosed on December 10, 1968, the Regents included Mrs. Randolph A. Hearst, Norman Chandler, Samuel B. Mosher, John E. Canaday, Philip L. Boyd, Norton Simon, William E. Forbes, William M. Roth, Mrs. Edward H. Heller, Frederick G. Dutton, William K. Coblentz, De-Witt A. Higgs, W. Glenn Campbell and so on. These people served on the boards of directors or as CEOs of The Hearst Foundation, Security Pacific National Bank, Western Bancorporation, Broadway-Hale Stores, First Surety Corporation, Stanford Bank, Commonwealth Assurance Corporation, Crown-Zellerbach Corporation, Pacific Lighting Co., and more than 20 other large corporations and utilities.[3]

---

2 The word, "troubleshooter," for Meese is borrowed from Bob Woodward's *Shadow: Five Presidents and the Legacy of Watergate.* (See his chapters on President Reagan's Irangate and Contragate.)

3 Including Arizona Bancorporation, Southern California Edison, Pauley Petroleum, Del Monte Foods, Irvine Foundation, DiGiorgio Company, Norton Simon Inc., the 230,000 acre Tejon Ranch Co., Safeway Stores, Bell Brand Foods, Dresser Industries, Pan American World Airways, Western Airlines, Air West, F.E. Young Construction Company, Kaiser Steel, Crucible Steel, Atcheson

The Regents were plugged into transnational corporations with subsidiaries in Europe, the Caribbean, Latin America, Africa and Asia. Their names symbolized Who's Who of the American Industrial Empire, with financial holdings and directorships in industry, agribusiness, mass media, financial institutions and defense and intelligence agencies.

The raw power and influence of the Regents extended beyond California. They were also owners or on the boards of directors of corporations that controlled such conservative media as: the Associated Press and King Features Syndicate, the *San Francisco Examiner*, *Saturday Review*, *US News and World Report* and Scholastic Publications. They also owned *McCall's*, *Redbook*, *Popular Science*, *Good Housekeeping*, *Avon Paperbacks*, *Harper's Bazaar*, and so on.

They held commanding positions in firms supported by military contracts such as the Lockheed Corporation, Stanford Research Institute, Brookings Institution, Institute for Defense Analysis, Communication Electronics Inc., Watkins-Johnson Co., Center for Strategic Studies, Asia Foundation and Hoover Institution on War, Revolution and Peace. Charles Hitch, President of UC and another member of the Regents, had previously been employed in military agencies and research institutes supported by the Pentagon before Robert McNamara appointed him Assistant Secretary of Defense.

During the Sixties and early Seventies, only the radicals questioned the conflicts of interest between the Regents and their ties to armaments industries and think tanks serving the Department of Defense and CIA. The

---

Topeka and Sante Fe Railway Company, Northern Pacific Railroad and other corporations.

Regents helped ensure that UCB faculties were celebrated as long as they didn't challenge the interests of their military-industrial empire. When these interests were critically spotlighted in the Sixties, however, the Regents seized the power to veto tenure recommendations—a power traditionally given to UC chancellors.

This veto power undoubtedly affected the outcome of one of the most notorious academic freedom cases occurring on the Berkeley Campus: the case of Tony Platt.[4] Despite favorable recommendations from two tenure review committees, Chancellors Roger Heyns and Albert Bowker made a preemptive strike: By steadfastly refusing to grant tenure to Platt, a faculty member in the School of Criminology, they saved the Regents from widespread condemnation and embarrassment. Their refusal also blocked the possibility for overturning the Regents in the courts.

Bowker, replacing Heyns as Chancellor in the fall of 1971, headed the on-campus team of assassins. Previously, he had been Chancellor of the City University of New York (CUNY) where his credentials attracted the UC Regents. For instance, the American Association of University Professors (AAUP) found that Bowker's office at CUNY had violated the principle of academic freedom when it dismissed three CUNY assistant professors on one campus and ten faculty members at another.[5]

---

4 An equally notorious case involved Ely Katz who was an assistant professor in the early Sixties. He had refused to cooperate with HUAC when it asked whether he had been a member of the Communist Party. He was fired from the university because he refused to answer the same question when UCB Chancellor Strong posed it. He then sued the university and forced it to rehire him. However, despite favorable recommendations from his tenure review committee and Dean, he was denied tenure.

5 *Bulletin of the American Association of University Professors.*

The first case involved a professor who had been an advisor to an SDS chapter. He had participated in sit-ins with two other dismissed colleagues. The second case involved faculty support for a "third world" student rights movement.[6]

In both instances, Bowker's administration employed shifting and dilatory tactics to cover-up the political purges. In the so-called case of the Ten, his administrators defended the dismissals by disclosing political documents from secret files compiled on the faculty.[7] Responding to the uproar over the dismissals, Bowker claimed that he had not conducted a political purge; instead, the faculty had been fired solely because they had misused their positions or had defects of moral character or were too incompetent to meet academic standards.[8] Besides, he said, a projected reduction in enrollment also had necessitated the reduction in the faculty. Yet when

---

1973. "Queensborough Community College (CUNY)," Vol. 59, No. 1. pp. 46–54 and *Bulletin of the American Association of University Professors.* 1974. "The City University of New York (SEEK Center)." Vol. 60, No. 1. pp. 67–81.

6 The students forced the resignation of a Director favored by Bowker. The Director told four of the 10 faculty, who had supported the students' rights movement, that he felt they no longer had a "constructive role" to play at the Center. Students, almost entirely African Americans and Puerto Ricans, then successfully fought to replace the Director with a 'third world' person.

7 For instance, the *AAUP Bulletin* mentions that a faculty member, who called for support of black workers at a Ford plant, wrote one document. Circulation of this information was legally irrelevant to their case and violated their academic freedom.

8 Since the case involved a mass firing, Bowker faced the possibility of legal action. He preempted this action by selecting three black faculty from the other faculty and rehiring them to teach courses he had previously said they weren't competent to teach.

enrollments did not decrease as expected, Bowker did not reinstate the people he had fired.[9]

In addition, the American Federation of Teachers (AFT) faculty union at Berkeley (Local 1474) reported that Bowker was hired to add support within the university system for Reagan's plan to oust Charles J. Hitch, President of the University of California (UC). Reagan believed that Hitch had not acted ruthlessly enough in combating the free speech, civil-rights and anti-war campus movements. To assure Reagan and conservative Regents that he was the man to replace Hitch and bring UC into line, Bowker, according to the AFT, operated a lobby effort in the state capital that rivaled and countered Hitch's.[10]

Sindler, the second member of the team, was dedicated to eliminating the so-called "core members" of anti-government and anti-racist movements on campus. Originally at Cornell, Sindler had been the head of a university commission appointed to define student relations to law enforcement. While at Cornell, he had been enraged by attempts to provide amnesty for African-American students faced with disciplinary charges after conducting a sit-in at Willard Straight Hall. During the night of the sit-in, these students, who belonged to the Black Power movement,[11] reportedly foiled fraternity members who

9 Jeff Moad, "Bowker's NY Past." *The Daily Californian* May 16 1974. p. 5. As indicated, the so-called 'incompetent' faculty were African Americans.

10 "UC Tie-Line." *University Guardian*, AFT Local 1474, March 1973, p. 6.

11 Students representing the Free Speech Movement (FSM) campus chapter joined the African American students after the initial sit-in had taken place. Cornell had the third largest SDS chapter in the country. For different perspectives and a chronology of the Cornell events, see Cushing Strout and David I. Grossvogel (eds.)

attempted to break into the Hall to attack them. Terrified by the break-in, the African-American students obtained arms to defend themselves. This move immediately risked a clash with the Ithaca police who would have employed deadly force to expel the students from the Hall.

Certainly, the memory of the vicious brutality targeting African-American student protesters at southern universities must have encouraged the Cornell administration to refrain from calling the police. A Cornell dean contacted the students and promised support for amnesty if the students left the Hall. After the students marched out, guns in hand, the dean asked the Academic Senate to recommend "reconciliation," without harm to the students, when the violations were considered. The Senate deliberations went through various stages until the faculty wisely voted for reconciliation, thereby blocking the threat of further demonstrations and deadly responses from police.

A diary kept by Sindler's department chair, Clinton Rossiter, tells how the reconciliation debate at Cornell took a nasty turn. Sindler, a foremost opponent of reconciliation, felt so strongly about the issue that he publicly threatened to resign if the Senate majority sided with the students. His opposition provoked a Black Power student leader to threaten him and his family in a radio broadcast.[12] Sindler rented a hotel room and left his fam-

---

Divided We Stand: Reflections on the Crisis at Cornell. New York: Doubleday 1970.

12 A student who thought the radio broadcast had not begun made the threatening comments (in an informal discussion with the announcer). His comments appear to have been couched in the exaggerated 'ghetto rhetoric' often employed by black power students regardless whether their own class backgrounds.

ily for a few nights. Rossiter, who was also threatened, did not leave his residence and no one harmed him or his family.[13]

Despite Sindler's efforts, the Senate approved the reconciliation measure and he resigned, leaving when his academic year was up. He accepted an offer from Berkeley where politically compatible administrators and colleagues supported his views.

Beginning in 1971, Sindler's name appeared on various UCB documents aimed at repressing campus radicals or curtailing their support among the faculty. A Senate committee that succeeded in expanding the rules for disciplining faculty who acted "against the interests of the university" issued some of these documents in February 1971. Another set of documents included the June 15, 1973 report (and various memos) by Sindler— who chaired Bowker's committee evaluating the School of Criminology. The committee report fabricated the so-called "indisputable facts" and ideological terrain on which the struggle over the school's fate emerged.

Still another document from May 30, 1972, reflected his anti-union sentiments and would have undermined Local 1474 of the American Federation of Teachers, the only UCB faculty organization that consistently opposed Reagan, Bowker and their cohorts throughout the 1970s. Throughout the late sixties and early seventies, Local 1474 had defended UCB employees against discrimina-

---

13 A number of other faculty members were threatened by the broadcast and they also spent a few nights at hotels because of their alarm. See Donald A. Downs, *Cornell '69: Liberalism and the Crisis of the American University*. Ithaca; Cornell University Press, 1999. Also, Caleb S. Rossiter. *The Chimes of Freedom Flashing: A Personal History of the Vietnam Anti-War Movement and the 1960s*. Washington DC: TCA Press 1996.

tory hiring policies as well as Reagan's budget cuts, administrative abuses and political persecution. Although the administration and its faculty allies—including Sindler—could not control the AFT Local, they finally attempted an end-run around it. They encouraged the Academic Senate to pass a resolution calling for the creation of a so-called "professional association" to "prepare for the eventuality of collective bargaining." Within days of the resolution's passage, Sindler and six other conservatives distributed the resolution among the UC Berkeley faculty and requested them to join up. Bowker was obviously involved in this conspiracy, because a "check-off" form with a UC seal, clipped to the resolution, allowed faculty members to automatically deduct membership dues from their earnings.[14] Ironically, this sordid enterprise was abandoned when California's Legislative Analyst, Alan Post, quickly recommended that funds for the Academic Senate be line-itemed to prevent any involvement in collective bargaining. Since the Senate was a state-funded agency, Post declared, it could not "participate directly or indirectly in collective bargaining."[15] To avoid conflict with the state legislature and courts, Sindler, his conservative cohort and the administration, abandoned their attempt to form a company union.

Sanford Kadish, a professor at the School of Law, was the third notable member of the assassination team. Kadish, it is important to note, headed the faculty "search committee" that recommended Bowker as the

---

14 The statement implicated administrative collusion because it informed the faculty that they could have their dues *automatically* deducted from their salaries. A check-off accounting department form was attached.

15 "Berkeley Faculty Association Threatens Senate Funding." *University Guardian*, AFT Local 1474, March 1973, p. 3.

new Chancellor. Although the *San Francisco Chronicle*, on February 28, 1971, dubbed Kadish "UC's Ethical Moderate,"[16] he was, in reality, a voice for the Regents who alleged that movement professors were "subverting the liberty" they were striving to protect.[17]

Also, Kadish believed trade unionism was antithetical to university aims and made the ridiculous claim in the *Chronicle* interview that pro-union professors undermined the university, considering themselves "employees first, and academics second." As student protests rocked the campus, he protested that Berkeley was not "a political battleground." Nevertheless, he insisted that conservatives "balance the liberals" when faculty committees were appointed. With Orwellian flair, he further declared that "extremists, students and many of the professors" were not entitled to academic freedom, because

16 Carl Irving, "What Worries Profs Most – Freedom, Tenure, Funds." *S.F. Sunday Examiner & Chronicle*, February 28, 1971. p. 10.

17 The *Chronicle* interviewer said Kadish "has been credited with averting extreme stands in such matters as the People's Park, the course involving Eldridge Cleaver and the demands of Third World Groups." In actuality, prior to being appointed Dean of the School of Law, Kadish helped neutralize the Academic Senate's obligation to uphold academic freedom – especially when it involved a conflict with the Regents. Kadish was AAUP Executive Committee chairperson at UCB when it was confronted in 1968, with an unprecedented ruling by the Regents that prevented the well-known sociologist, Troy Duster, and two other faculty members from holding an experimental course scheduling Eldridge Cleaver as an ongoing 'guest lecturer.' Kadish convinced the Committee and, then, the Academic Senate to adopt a resolution that vaguely supported academic freedom but abandoned the three faculty members who were jointly teaching the course and who had requested backing from the Senate. Schwendinger, who also was on the AAUP Executive Committee, resigned because the three faculty members were not supported.

they were "hacking away at the most precious asset on campus - an atmosphere of freedom."[18]

In this contentious environment, Bowker, Sindler and Kadish were participants in a counter-reformist alliance that suppressed students and faculty who (1) supported student participation in university management, (2) drafted legislative initiatives for a civilian police review board, (3) unmasked right-wing crime-fighting initiatives (4) advocated prison reforms and (5) opposed police brutality. The radicals who built this program were also primarily responsible for unprecedented changes in the racial and gender composition of students and faculty within the School. Taking charge of the Criminology admissions committee over a three to four year period, they actively recruited students from minority groups and women. Previously, instructors were virtually all white males. The radicals championed faculty-hiring policies that made unprecedented changes during the relatively short period when they were influential.[19]

Despite urgent student and faculty demands for affirmative action, these changes were by no means typical. In March 1973, for example, the AFT faculty union[20] published segments of the Health Education and Welfare Office of Civil Rights report dealing with women in academic positions.[21] The report accused the UCB adminis-

---

18 Carl Irving, op cit.

19 Platt and Schwendinger chaired the admissions committee during most of this period.

20 Although HEW gave the report to UC administrators, it refused to make it available to those who filed the complaint that led to the review. These administrators also refused to release the report on the grounds of pending legal action

21 Other segments, it pointed out, covered "Minorities in Academic Positions" and "Minorities and Women in Non-Academic positions."

tration of not complying with federal civil-rights mandates.[22] It especially singled out the Academic Senate whose membership reflected employment policies that discriminated against women and minorities.[23]. Other publications, such as *Public Affairs Report: Bulletin of the Institute of Government Studies*, showed that, in 1970, women comprised only 2.3 percent of all full professors at Berkeley. In 1973, the ratio had not improved; in fact, "larger proportions of women held lower positions lacking both tenure and status."[24] Three years later, in 1976, the Committee on Senate Policy reported to the Academic Senate that only a limited number of departments were treating the issue of gender discrimination seriously rather than taking refuge behind the myth that affirmative action is "counter-productive to the quest for excellence."[25]

The changes produced by the radicals went beyond

---

22 "UCB Stalls Affirmative Action Compliance" and "HEW Report on Women: 'UC Not In Compliance.'" *University Guardian*, March 1973, p. 4. The Local published some of the OCR findings, noting that the administration had refused to release these findings on the grounds of pending legal action. Litigation brought by the League of Academic Women alleging sex discrimination was being argued in court around that time.

23 The Senate review committees were either composed of people who supported the administration or who were split into factions of belligerent conservatives, ambivalent moderates and 'principled' liberals. While, as far as we know, there were no socialists in these committees, there were people like Paul Seabury, who was repeatedly attacked for ties to defense agencies, and Sindler.

24 *Public Affairs Report: Bulletin of the Institute of Government Studies* V. 14, December 1973, No. 6, p.2.

25 "Report of the Committee on Senate Policy State of the Campus Message, Meeting of the Berkeley Division," Monday, April 26, 1976.

the school. For instance, Takagi, who was at that time the first and only tenured Asian American social science professor at UCB, held the first Asian American Studies course in the United States. He helped municipal governments and police and probation departments introduce police training, cultural sensitivity training and research into the treatment of racial minorities. He was repeatedly asked by the community relations division in the Department of Justice to participate in training sessions, conferences, Law Enforcement Assistance Administration (LEAA) planning sessions, and so forth as an expert on affirmative action and racial discrimination. On one occasion, the director of the division, in his introductory comments reported that nine out of the 10 black criminologists with doctorates in the United States had graduated from "Paul Takagi's shop at Berkeley."[26] Also, largely due to affirmative action initiated by the radicals, the School of Criminology graduated at least 20 women with doctorates before it was closed down.

The UC Berkeley School of Criminology was targeted for additional reasons. It actually offered a politically balanced curriculum taught by conservative and moderate liberals as well as radical democrats. Out of about a dozen professors, for most of the period in question, only four were considered radicals and three of them did not have tenure.[27] The curriculum, as a whole, emphasized traditional professional courses; but the radicals initiated courses rarely offered by criminologists elsewhere. Barry Krisberg, Tony Platt and Paul Takagi, for example, reorganized the introductory course and pro-

---

26 Apparently, eight had doctorates but the ninth may not have completed his degree.

27 This would make five when Elliot Currie is included. He is the lecturer mentioned in the list of radicals but was an Acting Assistant Professor in the final years of the School.

vided radical as well as non-radical topics dealing with the causes, characteristics and control of crime.[28] They designed the course for students at large, attracting around 800 undergraduates eager to know what the field was about even when they were not interested in becoming criminologists. Like other criminology courses offered by the radicals, these instructors emphasized economic, political and social relations that determined the historical development of crime and criminal justice. In addition, Schwendinger taught theoretical courses on crime and delinquency and seminars on "instruments of discovery" that veered away from the blind empiricism and sterile survey methods dominating the field.[29]

Other members of the staff also contributed to this new beginning in learning. Elliot Currie, originally a lecturer and eventually an Acting Assistant Professor, played an important role in this regard. Drew Humphries and other female graduate students who taught courses also contributed. Faculty such as Aviva Menkes, Richard Korn, Lloyd Street and John Davis focused on racial and ethnic repression, crimes against women, civil liberties and reforms of the police and correctional institutions.

Contact with visiting professors such as Marie Bertrand, an outstanding feminist scholar from the University of Montreal; Richard Quinney, a pioneer in critical criminology; Alphonso Pinckney, a noted black

28 The course description, evaluation and readings can be found in the first edition of *Crime and Social Justice*. See Barry Krisberg, "Teaching Radical Criminology: Criminology 100A-B, Professors Barry Krisberg, Tony Platt, and Paul Takagi," *Crime and Social Justice*, 1974, 1 (Spring-Summer) 64-66.

29 This course among other things exposed students to ethnography, sociometrics, small group experiments, and the writings of Charles Pierce and other pragmatists interested in the development of scientific thinking.

sociologist from Hunter College; John Irwin, a trailblazer in penal studies; and David Du Bois, the son of W.E.B. Du Bois and editor of the Black Panther party's newspaper, expanded the new learning.

Speakers from labor organizations such as the United Farm Workers were invited to relate how police harassment and brutality repressed the unionization of migratory workers. Finally, the School was further enriched by campus-wide talks featuring speakers such as Ralph Nader, who excoriated "Crime in the Suites."

The radical faculty helped reorganize the undergraduate curriculum. They encouraged a systematic approach to criminology, encouraged internships in criminal-justice agencies and organized individual studies that catered to student interests. It was no secret that the curriculum had been influenced by this faculty but when the School was attacked virtually every course with socially critical content was labeled as "radical."

Despite their small number, this faculty generated a vibrant intellectual climate. Fundamental questions were raised about America, about its class, gender and racial inequality. And the interaction between radical students and faculty generated the "critical mass" that produced an Enlightenment-like explosion of rich theoretical ideas about the nature of crime and criminal justice.[30]

Some of the students educated by the radicals helped edit *Issues in Criminology*, publishing articles and interviews that would not have appeared in major

---

30 The originality of their work is missed in mainstream summaries of radical writings, which usually mistake English writings for American even though prominent radicals at Berkeley and elsewhere had gravitated toward political economy rather than sociology of deviancy (e.g., labeling theory), which had become fashionable at that time.

criminology journals. Interviews with pioneering Canadian and British scholars[31] and some of the earliest challenges to mainstream positions appeared there— including Gene Grabiner's attack on value-free science and state morality, Barry Krisberg's trenchant critique of a University of Pennsylvania training program for gang leaders, and Schwendingers' ground-breaking article on the legal definition of crime.[32] Critical historical studies included Melanie Fong and Larry D. Johnson's critique of the Eugenicist movement and institutionalized racism, Dorie Klein's exposé of sexism in theories of female criminality, Martin B. Miller's scrutiny of progressive-era prison reforms, John Pallas and Bob Barber's analysis on prison struggles, Tony Platt and Randi Pollock's article on public defenders, Joyce Clements' critique of the rhetoric of repression, Elliot Currie's article on medieval witch hunts and Richard Quinney's approach to legal order.

Racism in criminal justice was further targeted by John A. Davis' views of black men toward crime and law, Charles Reasons' study of prisoner's rights, Larry D. Trujillo's analysis of criminology literature on Chicanos, and Homer Yearwood's critique of police discrimination against blacks. In addition, in 1973, the editors of *Issues*[33] broke new ground by publishing an

---

31 Such as the University of Montreal feminist, Marie Bertrand, and three British criminologists, Ian Taylor, Paul Walton and Jock Young.

32 Thirty years later, in the introduction to *What is Crime?: Controversies over the Nature of Crime and What to Do about It* (Rowman & Littlefield) the editors, Mark M. Lanier and Stuart Henry, call the article "the classic counterstatement to the legal definition" of crime.

33 The editors included June Kress, Virginia Engquist Grabiner, Cynthia Mahabir, Wayne Lawrence, Eleanor Evans, Susan Barnes

entire edition devoted to women with articles by Dorie Klein, Meda Chesney-Lind, Kurt Weis, Sandra S. Borges, and Dale Hoffman-Bustamante.

The radical faculty published articles in *Journal of Marriage and the Family, Federal Probation, Social Problems, Issues in Criminology, Insurgent Sociologist, Crime and Social Justice* and so forth. Works by Platt and Schwendinger also appeared in anthologies such as the *Politics of Riot Commissions, 1917-1970,* and *Delinquency and Group Processes.*

Toward the end of the Sixties, a notable proportion of doctoral students began to conduct research that changed the School. Many students, of course, continued to adopt technocratic paradigms for studying crime, crime control or managerial problems, for instance. But Lynn B. Cooper's (1976) dissertation scrutinized the expansion of the "state repressive apparatus," spurred by the Law Enforcement Assistance Administration (LEAA). Richard C. Speiglman (1976) studied this expansion in California's prison hospital and his access to medical records exposed "new prison walls" based on the massive and unjustified use of tranquilizing drugs in treatment of *MDOs*, i.e., "Mentally Disordered Offenders."

Doctoral students also produced a penetrating series of historical police studies. Virginia Engquist Grabiner's (1976) research documented the repressive police tactics used against the militant members of the women's suffrage movement. Studies, by Joyce Clements (1975), Robert Mintz (1974) and Charles Keller (1974), investigated the economic and political factors behind the recurring employment of police forces to crush San Francisco maritime strikes, mine workers' unions and

---

and Tommie Hannigan.

Native Americans. Discarding a "great man theory" of policing, Michael Rustigan (1974) showed that Jeremy Bentham was not the sole catalyst for the creation of the early 19th century metropolitan police. Instead, the Benthamite movement in London successfully brought the first police force into being because London business interests backed it. Gregory Mark (1978) scrutinized the American imperial policies expanding the opium trade in China. Vast fortunes were made as American ships (e.g., the "China Clipper") transported tremendous quantities of opium from the near east to China. After British and American warships crushed China's attempt to block the trade, the "foremost families" of the nation, the Cabot, Cushing, Forbes, Surges, Peabody and Delano families, poured their drug fortunes into railroads and industry. We know from Mark's study that opium trafficking backed the rise of the greatest industrial power in the world.

Significant information about the origins of criminal justice appeared in other dissertations. James Brady (1974) described the centuries-long evolution of restorative "popular justice" in China while Gregg Barak (1974) probed the origins of the public defender system in the United States. Contrary to liberal explanations, the movement to establish a public defender system was not the outcome of progressive and humanitarian reform but rather part of a larger regulative movement occurring both inside and outside the criminal justice system.[34]

Some graduate students focused on feminist topics. Frances Coles (1974) examined the experiences of women lawyers while Julia Schwendinger's (1975) disserta-

---

34 It was also created to delegitimize critics of class-biased justice and to abolish requirement of 'rotation,' thereby unburdening corporate lawyers from defending indigents.

tion was devoted to the rape victim and her treatment by the justice system. Lynn Osborne (1973) and Drew Humphries (1973) dissected the politics of anti-homosexual and anti-abortion laws as well as the racial, gender and social class inequities in criminal justice agencies.

Race and crime was another topic. David Dodd (1972) examined the formation and disintegration of personal identity in urban Afro-America. George Napper (1971) researched the African American student movement and Llewellyn (Alex) Swan (1972) investigated the causes of race riots.

Tetsuya Fujimoto (1975) adopted ideas from political economy rather than social-control theory to explain low crime rates among Japanese immigrants who settled in California at the end of the 19th century. Unlike the crime rates among European immigrants who settled in Northeastern cities, these low rates were determined by the widespread involvement of Japanese immigrants in family farming rather than in industrial labor markets and their surplus labor force.

Robert E. Meyers (1974) showed how funds for Los Angeles parks and recreation programs were used to control the poor. During economically and politically volatile periods, the funds shifted dramatically from middle-class communities to working-class communities. But in "normal times," the LA government gave the lion's share of these funds to middle class communities.

Examination of social class and delinquency produced Anthony Poveda's (1970) and Joseph Weis' (1974) studies of working-class and middle-class communities.[35] Unlike simple-minded research encouraged

---

35 Stanley Friedman's (1969) Master's thesis is another one of

by delinquent-subculture and social-control theories, their fieldwork focused on complex relations connecting social classes, adolescent subcultures and delinquency.

The variety of critical studies at the School was simply extraordinary. As a result of these and other studies —such as Ronald Glick's (1969) dissertation on New Left organizers in a southern community and Renee Kasinsky's (1972) study of men who escaped the draft by settling in Canada—the graduate students helped broaden the research conducted today.

Furthermore, the intellectual achievements at the School did not end with dissertations. A faculty-student collective created an entirely new journal, *Crime and Social Justice*, devoted to radical criminology (Schwendingers 1999). The first edition featured articles on radical criminology, political origins of American prisons, prison movement in Scandinavia and a pioneering conference sponsored by European radical criminologists held in Florence, Italy, which had been attended by members of the collective.

The journal published "The Garrison State in a 'Democratic' Society" and "Rape Myths in Legal, Theoretical and Everyday Practice"—articles addressing the unwarranted number of racially biased killings by police and the questionable view of rape in criminology. Renamed *Social Justice: A Journal of Crime, Conflict & World Order*, the journal has continued to be edited by people originally associated with the School. The journal's 25th Anniversary Edition was published in the Fall of 1999.

The radicals published several books. Tony Platt and

---

these important early empirical contributions to the study of subcultures and delinquency.

Lynn Cooper edited *Policing America*, and radicals at the School who had formed a center for criminal-justice research wrote *The Iron Fist and Velvet Glove*, dealing with topics rarely covered in criminology, such as the police-industrial complex, police brutality, counterinsurgency and political repression.[36] The Schwendingers' *Sociologists of the Chair*[37] described the origins of corporate liberalism and the technocratic category, "*social control*," that dominated theoretical criminology.

The changes produced by the radicals went beyond the school. Julia Schwendinger, Tommie Hannigan, Suzie Dod and other women students joined with local Berkeley women to create the first anti-rape group in the United States, *Bay Area Women Against Rape*. These women forced Herrick Hospital authorities to remove the emergency room chief who treated victims like "pieces of meat" and pressured the institution to adopt medical protocols treating rape victims as human beings.[38] They established support programs and a telephone hotline for victims, issued community information bulletins and tacked "streetsheets" with descriptions of rapists and their *modus operandi* to telephone poles. After pressuring the Berkeley DA's office and Police Department, they instituted a victim-advocacy program for court cases and created sensitivity-train-

---

36 Tony Platt and Lynn Cooper, *Policing America*. Englewood Cliffs: Prentice-Hall, 1974. Also, Staff of the Research Center on Criminal Justice, *Iron Fist and the Velvet Glove: An Analysis of the U.S. Police*. Berkeley: Center for Research on Criminal Justice, 1975.

37 Herman and Julia Schwendinger. 1974. *Sociologists of the Chair: A Radical Analysis of the Formative Years of North American Sociology (1883-1922)*. New York: Basic Books, 1974.

38 To force compliance, the group actually prevented the hospital from receiving a federal grant.

ing sessions for police officers handling rape-victim cases. This vital organization and its programs are still active as we write.

Unprecedented activities sponsored by the radicals created a School that was not limited to producing technocratically oriented professionals. With the help of Cyril Robinson, Takagi and Schwendinger initiated discussions that led to the first radical criminology sessions at annual meetings of the American Society of Criminology.[39] Some students and faculty were servicing organizations and movements that were independent of the criminal-justice agencies and, in some cases, in conflict with them. The School, therefore, was providing assistance to elements in civil society that symbolized and fostered democracy.

---

39 Thanks, in part, to Charles Wellford's cooperation.

3 | Fighting "Friendly Fascists"

S ome criminologists stereotype the radicals as "extremists" and "utopians" with ultra-left aims. But most radicals at the School never fit this stereotype.

It is simply impossible to understand the radicals accurately without realizing that social movements—antiwar, civil rights, feminism—pulled them together despite their diverse positions and professional interests. Feminists, anarchists, social democrats, Maoists, left-liberals, moderate-liberals and people with no distinct political perspective were found among the radicals. And they certainly included utopians whose dreams at that time made life bearable.

Although many radicals finally organized themselves into professionally oriented task groups to sponsor a conference on prisons, launch a criminology journal and write a textbook or model legislation; and although one could find the same people drinking beer and dancing every Friday at an Irish Pub, *The Star and the Plough*, their networks were fluid and expanded or contracted depending upon what was happening outside the School. The networks interfaced social and political movements in the San Francisco Bay Area. And, until the School itself was in peril, most of their activities were characterized by short-term—often reactive and spontaneous—responses to events outside the school.

Yet a single strand tied these diverse people together. Despite their long hair, pony tails, beards, hippie argot, cowboy hats, Mao hats, headbands, tie-dyed shirts, miniskirts, and bongo drums—despite the revolutionary sloganeering (e.g. "Power to the People!") and posturing, the students and faculty who created the program so despised by Bowker, Sindler and Kadish were *radical democrats* whose members shared the same hatred of the war, political repression, police brutality and social inequality.[1] They believed their "new criminology" would advance equality, justice and "participatory democracy." They really did believe in what America was supposed to be. The majority still does.

Todd Gitlin's autobiography describes factional conflicts and terrorist groups that allegedly imploded the Students for a Democratic Society (SDS). But the Criminology radicals marched to the beat of a different drummer. They did not advocate the forcible overthrow of the United States government, and even the few who had a "romance with communism" never encouraged anyone to form a terrorist group like the Weathermen. Furthermore, the Criminology radicals were free of factional conflict and violence. Their direct actions relied on what had become standard forms of civil disobedience, which ignored university rules governing the conduct of demonstrations but avoided violence.[2] For instance, on June 6, 1974, *The Daily Californian* headlines declared, "100 Riot Policemen Dispersed Peaceful Haviland Hall

---

1 Deeds not words are the criteria behind this judgment.
2 Students violated these rules because they knew that they had no chance of getting anywhere with the administration by adhering to them.

Sit-In." To protest the closing of the School, students pushed campus police aside to gain entrance to Haviland Hall but conducted a nonviolent "sit- in."[3] When police massed in front of the building the next day directing their shot-guns and gas grenade launchers at a crowd of about 1,000, and commanded the students inside to leave, the students left peacefully.[4]

The inescapable truth is that the police were primarily responsible for the violence occurring throughout the Bay Area. Granted, some vandalism and arson were committed by a very small number of Berkeley students in the 1969 Third World Strike. Also, "crazies,"[5] as they were called, in antiwar demonstrations along Telegraph Avenue and Shattuck Avenues, indiscriminately smashed windows—including windows of merchants who *supported* the anti-war movement.[6] But this gratuitous, spontaneous and disorganized violence pales in comparison with the organized and systematic clubbing and beatings by the police.

For example, two years earlier, on October 18, 1967,

---

3 Criminology students like Richard Schauffler, in fact, stopped some students (who were not in the School) from throwing rocks or provoking violence. The "crazies" were largely composed of homeless youth who were camped in vacant Berkeley lots.

4 An individual posing as a Daily Californian reporter entered Haviland Hall during the sit-in; but he was expelled after he spread false information that could possibly have caused panic in the Hall. This *agent provocateur* was identified as Brian Meyers in the following edition of the *Daily Californian*.

5 The 'crazies' usually lived hand-to-mouth in the residential area or streets south of campus near Telegraph Avenue.

6 Some crazies even set fire to a couple of rooms in the basement of Stephens Hall because, to them, the words 'criminology' and 'repression' may have been synonymous. The basement included the Criminalistics laboratory and offices, a few graduate student offices and Schwendinger's data-processing office.

around 200 police officers in a rapidly advancing wedge formation kicked, clubbed and beat 4,000 unarmed and nonviolent demonstrators who were blocking the Oakland Induction Center. A *Wall Street Journal* article entitled, "Blue Power and Control of Mobs," quoted a policeman at the scene. He said the demonstrators "weren't allowed enough time to get away."[7] Most of the crowd tried to back off as the wedge advanced but could not move fast enough without trampling each other. "They handcuffed this guy," one demonstrator reported. "He started to move and they knocked him down. Then four policemen got on him and beat him unconscious." A girl who talked back to police "was molested in a most disgusting way by five policemen." A physician called the scene a "massacre." While going to the aid of an injured woman, he was hit by a policeman. After asking for the policeman's badge number, he was struck in the jaw. Paul Gorman, a United Press International photographer, said he was standing on the sidewalk as the police moved forward; nevertheless, he was clubbed and kicked repeatedly in the head. The beating continued even though he pointed to his camera and repeatedly shouted that he was a press photographer.

Charles R. Gain, Oakland's Chief of Police, defended his force's tactics even though they had dispersed the demonstrators effectively on the previous day by resorting to nonviolent mass arrest.[8] Gain remarked, "When we were confronted with the problem, it quickly became obvious that the only thing that would remove thousands of persons from the street was a wedge-type tactic."

---

7 Ronald A. Buel and Richard Stone, "'Blue Power' and the Control of Mobs," *The Wall Street Journal*, Friday, October 20, 1967.

8 The demonstrations had taken place during the "Stop the Draft Week" organized nationally by anti-war organizations.

Governor Reagan declared, "The police action—swift and effective—was in the finest tradition of California's law enforcement agencies." "Force will be used without hesitation in order to maintain law and order and to allow Federal officials to carry out their duties," applauded an *Oakland Tribune* editorial.

But the authors of the *Wall Street Journal* article questioned the police tactics. They interviewed the Dean of the Criminology School, Joseph Lohman, who had a Master's Degree in sociology and who had been Sheriff of Cook County and Treasurer of Illinois under Adlai Stevenson, and Gordon Misner, an ex-police chief and a San Jose State professor who at that time was a visiting professor at the School. The authors reported that Lohman was not at the demonstration but he felt that the police should have used nonviolent alternatives that had at times been used effectively in the "free speech" movement sit-in in 1964.[9] Misner also found the tactics ill advised. He suggested that the demonstration could have been easily defused by temporarily moving the Induction Center to the Oakland Army base. He added, "This may have resulted in a loss of face for the police, but there could have been less violence and demonstrators wouldn't stay long at any empty Induction Center that was suddenly without inductees for a day."

These technical criticisms were mild compared to the response from four faculty members and a graduate student from the Criminology School.[10] A letter published

---

9 Similar peaceful tactics were used during the initial days of 'Stop the Draft Week'

10 Criminology professors Gordon Misner, Richard Korn, Bernard Diamond and Herman Schwendinger as well as David Fogel, at that time a graduate student, signed the letter. Also, faculty from School of Social Welfare faculty signed the letter.

in the *Daily Californian*, signed by these members, condemned the police brutality outright.[11] It called the police "sadists" and demanded an end to police
"vengeance, brutality and terror." It said, the justification
for police brutality "is as old as dictatorship: 'In order to
enforce the law we must be free to violate it when our
opponents violate it'." Speaking as teachers and citizens,
the signers added: "The right to engage in law violation
to prevent crime is a contradiction—one cannot stop
crime by committing it. If this is done, crime merely becomes the exclusive province of the police and a society
of law and justice is destroyed from within, by its own
protectors."

These statements did not go quietly into the night. An
outraged response came immediately. Don Fach, President of the California Peace Officers Research Association, fired off a letter to Lohman, claiming that the
Oakland police had conducted themselves professionally
and that they had been commended because they hadn't
confused "necessary force with brutality." On the contrary, he accused the Criminology faculty of being unprofessional because they criticized the police. He said
their outrageous public statements undermined police attempts to block "government by mob rule" and belied
"the professional dedication of the School of Criminology to the basic tenets of law enforcement." He informed
Lohman that he was forwarding his complaint about the
School to California law enforcement agencies, Governor Ronald Reagan, University of California's Board of
Regents, the International Association of Chiefs of Police and the FBI's J. Edgar Hoover.[12]

---

11 Editorial. "Professors Protest Brutality." *The Daily Californian*,
   Thursday October 19, 1967. p.8.
12 Don Fach, "Letter to Joseph Lohman from the Peace Officers

Yet the FBI was as guilty as the Oakland police of abrogating the democratic rights of citizens. For instance, the FBI had forged letters and sent undercover agents to provoke dissension among these leaders, spreading rumors about Martin Luther King and others to discredit them. FBI memos and agents had instigated the Chicago police department, which assassinated Fred Hampton, a Black Panther leader. In Oakland, the Black Panther Party had started community self-help programs, a breakfast program for children and educational forums and classes. But these reformist changes did not safeguard their headquarters from FBI-backed police raids that planted weapons, stole precinct lists and vandalized offices.[13]

Constitutional transgressions also occurred in Berkeley. On one occasion Berkeley high-school students, during lunchtime, joined a peaceful anti-war demonstration. They marched down University Avenue until a police cordon blocked their way. They were ordered to disperse, and tried, but found that police had blocked the streets in front, behind and to either side. After milling around, perplexed and terrified, police bullhorns informed the teen-agers and adults that they were being arrested for refusing to disperse. The marchers were herded into an empty lot where police fingerprinted hundreds of people *en masse*. (Busses for these people and trucks for the unloaded fingerprinting equipment had

Research Association of California," November 24, 1967. (This letter was distributed by Lohman to faculty and staff on December 5, 1967 to get their reactions before he drafted his reply.) Fach also demanded that Dean Lohman publicly repudiate the statements in the *Wall Street Journal* and *The Daily Californian*.

13 For the FBI covert campaign against political dissidents, see Brian Glick's *War At Home: Covert Action Against U.S. Activists and What We Can Do About It*. Boston: South End Press.

been parked *prior to the demonstration* on the side of the lot.) The teen-agers were then separated from the adults and, even though they were bussed to a juvenile detention facility in another city, San Leandro, the police made no attempt to inform parents that their children had been arrested, transported and imprisoned miles away.[14]

Going back in time, we should remember that University demonstrations evolved from "direct-action" tactics adopted by the civil rights movement in the South, where the "rule of law" brutally enforced racial segregation. When Berkeley "freedom fighters" returned. they applied various "direct-action" tactics learned in the South. The University tried to stop civil-rights and anti-war organizing on campus after *The East Bay Oakland Tribune*, targeted previously by student participation in an equal-opportunities campaign, denounced the campus organizers.[15] UCB authorities, goose-stepping behind the *Tribune*'s banner headlines, demanded that political activities cease and that tables with civil rights and an-

14 Leni Schwendinger was in that demonstration and we were terrified when she failed to return from school. Finally, a parent whom we telephoned discovered where the children were taken. We found on arrival at San Leandro that most of the children had gone home. Their parents were called after their children had signed a statement promising not to participate in demonstrations again. But Leni was in a small remaining group that bravely refused to sign the unconstitutional statement.

15 The direct-action tactics were first used to combat labor market discrimination in the San Francisco Bay area. During the academic year of 1963-64, Berkeley's CORE launched an equal employment opportunities campaign. Students joined the picketing, sit-ins and 'shop-ins' to force local merchants and newspapers to hire racial minorities. These activities culminated in the SF Sheraton Palace Hotel demonstration, when 2,000 students violated a court order restricting the number of pickets and 800 were arrested.

ti-war literature be removed from the Sather Gate area. The University is an educational institution, President Clark Kerr pontificated. "It should not be used as a base to organize and undertake direct action in the surrounding community." The Regents, of course, backed Kerr. Regent Frederick Dutton demagogically declared, "Our society believes in law and order but also in freedom."[16]

Students defied the ban on political activities. They condemned President Kerr for surrendering to businessmen, including the right-wing *Tribune* publisher, former U.S. Senator William Knowland. Between 1000 and 1500 people occupied Sproul Hall, the administration building. The police were called to clear the building and, when the arrests occurred, 773 students were booked. A civil-rights attorney who accompanied the students and was arrested indicated that this was the first time police also charged students who had gone limp with resisting arrest because they refused to leave the building on their own volition.

After the Sproul Hall sit-in and arrests, the students called a university-wide strike. Students laughed defiantly when a fellow-student, Mario Savio, announced, "Some of our best faculty were forced to leave during in the 1950 loyalty oath controversy. Some of our best students may be expelled now." The administration finally relented, even though it had attempted to suspend students cited for setting up literature tables and organizing around Sather Gate. Refusing to accept the suspensions, thousands of students joined the militants. Their added support overrode opposition from fraternity leaders and

---

16 *University Bulletin: A Weekly Bulletin for the Staff of the University of California,* Vol. 16, Number 13, October 30 1967, p. 1.

Young Republicans[17] and gave birth, in 1964, to the Free Speech Movement (FSM). Eventually, the authorities were forced to accept "time, place and manner rules" allowing students to organize politically, disseminate information and hold demonstrations—albeit with some restrictions.

The Regents, of course, never accepted the concessions won by the FSM. Nor was the administration willing or able to change its mind. Savio on one occasion reported, "We asked Kerr to get something more liberal out of the Regents, and the answer we got from this well-meaning liberal was the following: 'Would you ever imagine the manager of a firm making a statement publicly in opposition to his Board of Directors?'"

Earlier, when the conflict between the FSM and university authorities began to escalate, Kerr had called a press conference on October 6, 1964, and said, "Experienced on the spot observers estimated that the hard core group of demonstrators . . . contained at times as much as 40 per cent off-campus elements. And, within that off-campus group, there were persons identified as being sympathetic with the Communist Party and Communist Causes."[18] But the FSM was not deceived by Kerr's red herring. McCarthyism simply didn't work anymore.

Because Kerr's supporters on the faculty did not control the Academic Senate, he got the Council of Department Chairmen to back his decision to punish the protesters. He then attempted to use the Council to usurp the Senate's authority: The day before the Senate met, he

---

17 Max Heirich, *The Beginning: Berkeley 1964*. New York: Columbia University Press. pp. 198-99. The ASUC Senate condemned the strike and set up a counter-FSM organization, called *University Students for Law and Order*.

18 Heirich, op. cit. p. 196.

held a university-wide convocation attended by thousands of students at the Greek Theatre, the campus amphitheater.[19] There, flanked on the Greek Theatre stage by all the department heads, he ceremoniously accepted a Council resolution urging him to pursue judicial proceedings against the FSM. Professor Robert Scalapino, head of the political-science department, chaired the convocation and refused to allow FSM spokesperson Mario Savio to speak.[20]

The FSM supporters, who occupied most of the middle section and grassy knoll at the top of the huge amphitheater, roared with disapproval. They booed Kerr when he declared, "The University Community shall be governed by orderly and lawful procedures in the settlement of issues; and the full and free pursuit of educational activities on this campus shall be maintained." Such liberal platitudes at that point evoked anger rather than applause. Scalapino also inflamed the students when he expressed his resolute dedication to the preservation of freedom under law. Scalapino's remarks astonished students because he was a Southeast Asia expert who had been repeatedly implicated in servicing the CIA, Department of Defense and State Department—all of whose activities appeared to be violating constitutional and international laws.

Despite Scalapino's refusal to let him speak as the FSM representative, Savio tried to respond to Kerr's vows to punish the protesters. But he was arrested as he moved toward the stage. Pandemonium broke out. He was finally released and, to forestall a riot, was allowed to tell the audience that a rally would be held immediate-

---

19 This resolution was submitted by a faculty group, called the "Committee of 200."

20 No one was to speak except Scalapino himself and Kerr.

ly after the meeting. Nearly 10,000 people jammed Sproul Plaza for the rally at which FSM leaders urged the students to continue the strike. The Greek Theatre convocation had been a disaster for the administration and its faculty supporters.

The FSM disbanded after free speech was won; but it was temporarily reactivated by the administration's attempt to repress a small group of individuals who insisted on using the campus as an arena for expressing their right to use obscene words in public. The FSM leaders felt they had to back these students even though comparisons with their fight, in that context, belittled the gravity of the FSM's political aims. The mass media, however, had a field day: It convinced the California electorate that the FSM, whose name was now converted to the "Filthy Speech Movement," was comprised of irresponsible individuals who defied traditional values. The Regents entered the fray and Ronald Reagan— known later as the "Teflon" president, because of his ability to survive awful scandals—capitalized on this incident by promising the electorate to clean up "the mess" in Berkeley.

Despite these threats, the FSM movement was reproduced at other UC campuses, where students were equally impervious to McCarthyism and the hypocritical morality of administrators and politicians. A 1967 United States Senate Internal Security Subcommittee's report on Communist Activity, for instance, attributed the student protests at UC Los Angeles to a Communist plot, aimed at undermining troops in Vietnam. Nonetheless, the report "attracted more of a yawn than a yell from leaders on campus," according to the student newspaper, *UCLA Daily Bruin*. Ross Altman, leader of the campus chapter of SDS, said the government was trying to "define all revolution, organizing or protesting out of existence by calling it Communist." Mike Zeli, former editor of the *Daily Bruin*, sarcastically added, "As a member of the 'Left' I'm insulted that the Communists are getting all the credit for what we do."[21]

As anti-war activities took priority, a UCB teach-in was scheduled to encourage participation in the "Stop the Draft Week" demonstrations. To block the teach-in, Alameda County supervisors got a court injunction banning the use of university property advocating draft law violations.[22] But the ban backfired. Thousands of students were once more ready to defend the right to organize on campus to support off-campus activities, including civil disobedience. On Monday, the first day of "Stop the Draft Week," 6000 students protested the war at an unofficial rally in Sproul Plaza. On "bloody Tuesday," 3,000 students—including criminology students—joined other demonstrators to shut down the Oakland Induction Center. By Thursday, more than 10,000 demonstrators were defying the police. Up to and including Friday, students were defending themselves against the police violence by showing up with helmets, gas masks and shields. They pushed automobiles into the streets leading to the induction center and punctured tires to block busloads of inductees.[23] Police chased "mobile units" of students that would suddenly disperse and then reform at prearranged locations to renew attempts to halt the Center's operation.

By 1969, student movement demands at Berkeley had

---

21 "Campus Reaction: Reds on Campus Report – 'unsuccessful' 'irresponsible.'" *UCLA Daily Bruin*, Summer Edition, Thursday 23, 1966, p. 1.

22 This law was the Universal Military Training and Service Act.

23 Many shields were made of garbage can lids.

increased. Feminist, Asian and Black Power movements urged the creation of an ethnic studies department and implementation of affirmative action for women and third-world people in student admissions and faculty hiring, especially for professional schools.[24] The Black Power movement raised the ante, calling for the creation of a black college. The anti-war movement denounced the Reserve Officer Training Corps (ROTC) program. It discredited faculty who supported nuclear-weapons development[25] or who were consultants and researchers for the CIA, State Department and Department of Defense (DOD) such as Irving Teller, Paul Seabury and Robert Scalapino.[26] The movement demanded an end to DOD-sponsored research.

---

24 For example, in 1970, women comprised only 2.3 percent of all full professors at Berkeley. In 1973, the ratio had not improved. In fact, "larger proportions of women held lower positions lacking both tenure and status." (*Public Affairs Report: Bulletin of the Institute of Government Studies* V. 14, December 1973, No. 6, p.2). Three years later, in 1976, the Committee on Senate Policy reported to the Academic Senate that only a limited number of departments were treating the issue of gender discrimination seriously rather than taking refuge behind the myth that affirmative action is "counter-productive to the quest for excellence." (*Report of the Committee on Senate Policy State of the Campus Message, Meeting of the Berkeley Division*, Monday, April 26, 1976.

25 In *Berkeley at War in the Sixties*, New York: Oxford University Press, p. 169, an historian, W. J. Rorabaugh notes: "No other university conducted so much government sponsored nuclear research, required its regents to deal with so many matters requiring security clearances, or found it necessary to seal permanently a room in a campus building after it was contaminated with radioactive material,"

26 Scalapino and Seabury's active support of the administration against the FSM was undoubtedly motivated by anti-war denunciations throughout the Vietnam War period.

A generation that did not live through this historical period may not fully understand how horrible and depraved the United States leadership was in dragging the country into the War. For example, President Johnson's attempt to make North Vietnam the culprit did not fool many students at that time. Previously, he had gotten Congress to back his undeclared war because of a supposed attack by North Vietnam on an American warship[27] He then sent the first combat units—two battalions of Marines—into South Vietnam to protect the Danang airbase from Northern forces who had allegedly infiltrated the South. However, the Tet Offensive in 1968 showed how deceitful he had been. Over 70,000 Vietcong troops—the armed forces of the National Front for the Liberation of South Vietnam (NLF)—had launched the Offensive and had attacked 100 South Vietnamese cities. Although they cooperated with Northern forces, these troops were not under Northern command. In fact, McNamara eventually confessed that the Tet Offensive was actually launched *against* the advice of North Vietnam.

Since the Tet Offensive, despite its magnitude, had taken the United States by surprise, it demonstrated that the military had grossly underestimated its enemy. It also showed that the United States government had misinformed the public about possible costs in American lives. While many Americans shared racist and nationalist sentiments that made them indifferent to Vietnamese

27 Congress passed the Gulf of Tonkin Resolution, which gave Johnson defacto approval even though the war remained undeclared. McNamara later confessed that the Naval vessel might not have been attacked; its officers may have interpreted matters incorrectly. See Robert S. McNamara, *Argument Without End : In Search Of Answers To The Vietnam Tragedy*. New York: Public Affairs, 1999, p. 167.

deaths, they were concerned about American casualties. The war no longer appeared winnable without unacceptable cost. Furthermore, no quick fix seemed available. International sentiments and the Soviets prevented the employment of American nuclear weapons, and sending Americans into North Vietnam promised to bring China into the war. It portended losses as large or larger than those incurred in North Korea when the Chinese overwhelmed American troops and forced them from the Manchurian border back to the 38th parallel.

To understand the increasing outrage felt by anti-war students, the government did not stop at this point. In the aftermath of the Offensive, the United States military deployed conventional weapons of mass destruction. It resorted to massive bombing runs aimed at annihilating the civilian support for the NLF. American forces targeted North Vietnam as well. Because it had unsurpassed technological superiority and could employ its air power without politically significant losses, the United States dropped more bombs on Vietnam (a country smaller than France) than had been dropped in the European and Mediterranean Theatres throughout the whole of the Second World War.[28] From 1967 through 1969, about four-and-a-half-million tons of bombs were dropped— about 500 pounds of bombs for every man, woman and child in Vietnam.

---

28 This estimation does not include artillery. After analyzing US ordinance reports, Noam Chomsky says, "The total number of artillery shells fired by US troops in South Vietnam in 1966 exceeded those fired by US forces during the whole of the Second World War." See, Bertrand Russell Peace Foundation Ltd., 1971, *Prevent the Crime of Silence: Reports from the sessions of the International War Crimes Tribunal founded by Bertrand Russell.* (Eds.) Peter Limqueco and Peter Weiss (with additional material selected and edited by Ken Coates and a Foreword by Noam Chomsky).

The devastation wrought by the United States was astounding. According to the Bertrand Russell War Crimes tribunal held in Sweden and Denmark, ferocious bombing in 1966 targeted North Vietnam's major cities such as Haiphong, Vinh, Nam Dinh, Viet Tri and Thai Nguyen. Against Hanoi, the Northern capital, the Americans dropped countless antipersonnel bombs that each released several hundred pellets to kill or wound all living creatures within two-thirds of a square mile—even in the most densely populated parts of the city. Twenty-five provincial cities were bombed—six of which were completely razed. The city of Dong Hoi—covering an area of 3.2 sq. kilometers, and with 16,000 inhabitants—was bombed 396 times, including 160 night attacks. Of the 110 district centers, 72 were bombed, leaving 12 of them left in ruins and 25 completely destroyed.

Such bombing, as indicated, was not restricted to the North. In the South, civilians and their social and economic infrastructure were also hit. Schools, hospitals, clinics and churches were bombed. High explosive bombs, fragmentation bombs, napalm bombs and antipersonnel bombs pounded regions occupied by the Vietcong. United States forces dropped herbicides and so-called "defoliants" that destroyed hundreds of thousands of farming acres. Meanwhile, United States troops on the ground threw suffocating "tear gases" and other chemical weapons into shelters and underground tunnels where women and children hid from bombs and artillery shells. This country's South Vietnamese allies used poison gas as well. On returning from a session with President Johnson and his advisors in 1967, John Naughton, an Assistant Secretary of Defense, admitted: "We seem to be proceeding on the assumption that the way to eradicate the Vietcong is to destroy all the village structures,

defoliate all the jungles, and then cover the entire sur-
face of South Vietnam with asphalt."[29]

Unfortunately, neither the Nuremberg Tribunal nor
the Geneva Conventions provided unequivocal standards
for determining whether the civilian casualties would
represent collateral damage or war crimes. For example,
the chief prosecutor at Nuremberg, General Telford Taylor (1972: 208), noted in *Vietnam an American Tragedy*,
that Nuremberg (and Tokyo) precedents would not have
prohibited the aerial bombardment of Vietnam. Amazing
as it may seem, these precedents did not necessarily por-
tray this kind of warfare as a crime. The Allies who administered the Nuremberg trials and their victor's
justice, relying on the mitigating standard of "military
necessity," had never considered the bombing of Dresden, Tokyo, Hiroshima and Nagasaki as war crimes.
How then could Nuremberg justifiably be used to condemn the bombardment of Hue or Hanoi, for instance?
Of course, Taylor granted that military necessity could
hardly be invoked for Dresden just when the Russians
were poised to seize the city or Nagasaki when surrender
negotiations were virtually over.[30] But Arthur "Bomber"
Harris, who ordered the British and American bombers
to drop 650,000 incendiary bombs and high explosives
on Dresden (producing a firestorm that immolated or as-
phyxiated more than 35,000 civilians) and the American
politicians and generals who ordered the atom bomb that
killed more than 100,000 civilians in Nagasaki, were
never put on trial at Nuremberg.

---

29 Quoted in Hitchens, *The Trial of Henry Kissinger*, p. 28-29.

30 Both of these were "open cities" and, because they lacked
military targets; were only lightly defended. Moreover, the
railroad yard and Shell Oil tanks in Dresden, which might have
been considered military targets, were not bombed.

Still, during the "25 days of horror" inflicted in March 1968 in response to the Tet Offensive, United States bombers reduced Hue, a city occupied by the Vietcong, to rubble. Further atrocities—such as the My Lai massacre and the systematic torture and execution of political dissenters and prisoners of war—demonstrated how far United States troops and their South Vietnamese allies were willing to go in violating elementary rules of war. The "carpet bombing," "free fire zones" and "search and destroy" missions employed by the United States were comparable to the genocidal warfare conducted by Europeans and their descendants against Native Americans in North America.

United States campaigns were also comparable to crimes committed by Nazi Germany in occupied nations. The NLF controlled most of the territory of South Vietnam.[31] To wrest territorial control, the US forcibly depopulated NLF regions through so-called "pacification campaigns." After investigating the "pacification" of Kien Hao in the Mekong Delta, for instance, Kevin Buckley, a Saigon bureau chief for Newsweek, disclosed:

> All the evidence I gathered pointed to a clear conclusion: a staggering number of noncombatant civilians – perhaps as many as 5,000 according to one official – were killed by US firepower to 'pacify' Kien Hoa. The death total there made the My Lai

---

31 The Pentagon Papers, discussed in Chapter 5, showed that the insurgents would have won a democratic election if the US had not sabotaged the 1954 Geneva settlement and cease-fire agreement between the French and Vietminh (which represented insurgents throughout Vietnam).

massacre look trifling by comparison. [32]

After terrorizing and killing people in these regions, the US forcibly relocated tens of thousands of men, women and children in detention camps near urban centers. Simultaneously, secret CIA operations such as the Phoenix Program assassinated over 20,000 suspected NLF guerrillas, many of them innocent civilians.

As these appalling events came to light, the anti-war movement exploded. The first national "Mobilization Against the War" committee (MOB) was formed in 1966. In the spring of 1967, Martin Luther King, Jr. led nearly half-a-million anti-war protesters from Central Park to the United Nations headquarters in New York City. Another 145,000 demonstrated outside a New York City foreign policy banquet addressed by Secretary of State Dean Rusk. Demonstrations erupted in other cities as the Defense Department announced its plans to increase the numbers of US troops in Vietnam. By the end of the year, more than half-a-million Americans were fighting in Vietnam.

The anti-war movement at UC Berkeley replaced the FSM as the chief organizing center of political dissent. A student Mobilization Committee Against the War was also established that year. This Committee did not confine itself to McNamara's "dirty war" in Southeast Asia. [33] Voices were also raised against crimes committed

---

32 Quoted in Hitchens, op cit. p. 31.

33 Anyone still convinced that the Vietnam War was justified should read McNamara's recollections, published in 1999. He called the war 'a mistake.' He said (p.22) it was started by the US because he and other government leaders believed in the 'domino theory,' which never proved true, and because they had *wrongly* believed North Vietnam leaders were Soviet puppets. What they actually found, was "a war in the South [Vietnam] that was

in Africa and other parts of the world. The State Department and CIA had created monsters such as Idi Amin in Uganda and General Mobutu in Zaire while subverting, imprisoning or killing national-liberation leaders including Patrice Lumumba in the Congo, Kwame Nkrumah in Ghana and Nelson Mandela in South Africa. Intelligence agencies and United States military policies had propped up or installed homicidal regimes in Southern Rhodesia, Portuguese Angola, Mozambique, Guinea-Bissau and South Africa.

Some links between the Berkeley faculty and the harms committed by government agencies turned out to be extraordinary. While the United States secretly armed the Indonesian military, for instance, one Berkeley faculty member, Guy Pauker, was a consultant for a CIA-subsidized "think tank," the Rand Corporation. Pauker urged his contacts in the Indonesian military to assassinate President Sukarno because his policy of "national conciliation" included the Indonesian Communist Party (PKI). The CIA helped destabilize the Indonesian economy as a result of an official State Department recommendation in 1962, which Pauker helped write. Then a special Military Training Advisory Group was set up in Jakarta to set the stage for the 1965 assassination and coup. Finally, Suharto, the dictator installed by the military, ruthlessly initiated what the CIA itself has called "one of the worst mass murders in the 20th century." Almost a million Indonesians were massacred. During the slaughter, observers reported rivers running with blood, filled with corpses of men, women and children, killed because they were family or friends of people supporting the PKI.[34]

_____

fundamentally a war among southerners" (p. 418).

34 Scott, Peter Dale. 1985. "The United States and the Overthrow

Furthermore, other Berkeley faculties were accused of conducting chemical and biological warfare research. In 1969, for example, the UCB Radical Student Union (RSU) published information on the Naval Biological Laboratory (NBL), which was administered by the School of Public Health (SPH) under terms of a contract between the UCB Regents and the Office of Naval Research (ONR). It listed, among other principal investigators at ONR, Sanford Elberg, Professor of Public Health and Dean of Berkeley's Graduate Division. (Incidentally, Elberg helped determine the fate of the Criminology School's graduate program.)[35] In 1961, NBL-ONR had sponsored the 1st International Symposium on Aerobiology, including artificial airborne transmission of anthrax and primary pneumonic plague, which is more infectious and virulent than the bubonic plague. The 2nd Symposium was sponsored by Fort Detrick, the Army Center for biological warfare research.

---

of Sukarno, 1965–67." *Public Affairs*, 58 (Summer) pp. 239–264. See Gabriel Kolko, *Confronting the Third World: United States Foreign Policy, 1945–1980* (New York: Pantheon, 1988), 180–191; Kathy Kadane, "US Officials' Lists Aided Indonesian Bloodbath in '60's," *Washington Post* (May 21, 1990): A5; and Roger Kerson, "The Embassy's Hit List," *Columbia Journalism Review*, 29 (November-December 1990): 9–14. A leading Indonesian security official, Admiral Sudomo, has given an estimate of around 500,000. See Robert Cribb, ed., *The Indonesian Killings*, 1956 (Clayton, Victoria: Monash Asia Institute, 1990), esp. 7–14. According to former CIA agent John Stockwell, the CIA estimated the total death toll from the anticommunist killings at 800,000; *Harper's* (September 1984): p.42.

35 The RSU listed six professors and lecturers from the School of Health who worked on projects connected with the NBL as researchers and administrators. It also noted that NBL conducted research for Fort Detrick. See Radical Student Union, *The Uses of UC Berkeley: Research*. Berkeley: RSU 1969, pp. 21-30.

It may be hard to believe that any faculty member on the UCB campus would be involved in this anti-human enterprise. Nevertheless, Theodore Rosebury, Professor of Bacteriology at the University of Illinois and former chief of airborne infection project at Fort Detrick, reportedly observed, "It's clear to anyone in the field that they're doing Chemical and Biological Warfare research at Berkeley."[36]

How in the world could the most conscientious Criminology students and faculty, whose very subject was crime, remain silent in the face of these developments? These people participated in one demonstration after another, especially as war crimes committed in Vietnam came to light.[37] One such crime especially stands out. The men, women and children inhabitants of My Lai, a Vietnamese village, for instance, had been massacred in 1968 by American troops who were ordered to destroy the village and everything in it. Even though the troops landing by helicopter outside the village were never confronted by enemy fire, the villagers were mowed down and their homes burned to the ground. Reports noted that bodies of men, women and children were lying everywhere. Just outside the village, a correspondent who witnessed the killing, reported, "There was this big pile of bodies. This really tiny little kid—he had only a shirt on, nothing else—he came over to the pile and held the hand of one of the dead. One of the GIs behind me dropped

---

36 Ibid.

37 Photographs and descriptions of these atrocities were repeatedly disclosed by the mass media. In addition, the Vietnam Veterans Against the War in 1972 published an inquiry into American war crimes (*The Winter Soldier Investigation*, New York: Beacon Press) that contained eyewitness accounts from 80 Vietnam veterans of such things as torture and executions of prisoners of war and the rape and slaughter of civilians.

into a kneeling position, 30 meters from this kid, and killed him with a single shot."[38]

Finally, the radicals were revolted by the hypocrisy, corruption and "high crimes and misdemeanors" exhibited at top levels of government. President Nixon was guilty of impeachable offenses—not because he had sex with an intern—but because he sanctioned illegal suppression of political opponents and requisitioned burglaries, illegal phone taps, money laundering and other criminal activities aimed at subverting political dissent and democratic elections. Vice President Spiro Agnew, who was eventually convicted of bribe taking, repeatedly posed with Nixon as a champion of "law and order." As the Criminology School was being set up for the kill, the former UC Regent, H.R. Haldeman, and Attorney General John N. Mitchell were spilling the beans about their involvement in the Watergate Conspiracy.[39]

Certainly, many at the School were not radicalized by these events. Certainly, some students and faculty objected to those who were because they themselves supported the war. Still others who were fearful or apolitical went no farther than signing a petition or complaining that the radicals interfered with their careers or education. Reminded years later about their responses,[40] we recalled a story told about Ralph Waldo Emerson and his friend, Henry David Thoreau, who had been jailed for

---

38 The Army suppressed both the photographs taken by Ron Haeberle (*LIFE*, December 5, 1969), who also accompanied the landing, and an eyewitness account for 12 months before Joseph Eszterhas, a *Cleveland Plain Dealer* reporter, exposed the massacre in 1969.

39 Mitchell was Attorney General from 1969-72. He was disbarred in 1975 after conviction in the Watergate case.

40 See, for example, Geis, op. cit. and Morn, op. cit.

opposing the war against Mexico by refusing to pay taxes. On seeing Thoreau behind bars, Emerson exclaimed, "Henry, what are you doing in there?" Thoreau replied, "What are *you* doing out there?"

4 | "Pigs Off Campus!"

During the "Third World Strike," when the Asian, Hispanic and Black Power movements attempted to force concessions from the university administration, sociologist Rodney Stark wrote,

> Police periodicals, pamphlets, and manuals, as well as the pronouncements of prominent police spokesmen, are unanimous in attributing the student demonstrations to a sinister and subversive conspiracy.[1]

He observed that the most widely cited and "authoritative" police report on the 1964 FSM activities at Berkeley had been prepared with the aid of then Berkeley Police Chief Addison H. Fording and published in the *Police Chief*, the official publication of the International Association of Chiefs of Police. This report attributed the FSM demonstrations to the "guiding hand of communists and extreme leftists."[2]

Still, to fully appreciate how the police responded to

---

1 Rodney Stark, "Protest+Police=Riot," In (Eds.) James McEvoy & Abraham Miller, *Black Power and Student Rebellion*, Belmont California: Wadsworth publishing Co. 1969, pp. 167-96.

2 April 1965, p. 10.

dissidents at Berkeley, we can compare it to a case in which Cornell President James A. Perkins, at great cost to himself, defied Sindler and his coterie. Despite unlawful acts by Black Power Cornell students, Perkins did everything possible to keep the police off campus. The Cornell situation was well known to students on other campuses. When this case is kept in mind, it will be easier to grasp student reactions to police at UC Berkeley.

OPERATING PRINCIPLES & MORAL CONFLICTS

While constructing an ideological defense for disciplining students at Cornell, Sindler and his coterie formulated two important moral rationales. The first rationale centered on the so-called threat to academic freedom posed by anti-war and Black Power movements. The anti-war movement unintentionally triggered this type of rationale when Averell Harriman, the United States ambassador to South Vietnam, came to speak at Cornell. Prior to his appearance, around 3000 students and faculty members had attended Cornell's first teach-in on the war. When Harriman arrived, the anti-war protestors disrupted his speech, deprived him of the microphone and insulted him as an imperialist agent. Although students did not relate this incident to academic freedom, faculty opposed to the disruption justified their stand on this ground.[3] Faculty considered the disruption of Harriman's speech a clear violation of academic freedom.

This faculty added "the rule of law" to their rationales for disciplining the protesters. As students (and some faculty) continued to break university rules of conduct by disrupting the annual review of the ROTC, blocking

---

3 Donald Alexander Downs, *Cornell '69: Liberalism And The Crisis Of The American University.* Ithaca: Cornell University Press, p. 37.

Marine recruiters, and so on, the university judicial system lost its legitimacy with many at the university. In
light of the great harms committed in the Vietnam War,
protesters believed that university disciplinary actions
against their "direct actions" were immoral. Still, while
protesters took this stand to achieve a higher moral end,
the advocates of law-and-order eventually demanded the
defense of the rule of law—by police if necessary.

The conflict at Cornell intensified as draft boards vin-
dictively reclassified students who openly protested the
war. When students burned draft cards in anti-war
demonstrations, their names were supplied to the boards
by Cornell proctors. Bruce Dancis, a Cornell undergraduate, was the first SDS member in the nation to destroy
his draft card; and his act galvanized resistance to the
war throughout the country. Meanwhile, the Johnson administration began to retaliate on a national level against
students by removing their draft deferments if they participated in anti-war demonstrations. These events
blurred the distinction between preservation of "the rule
of law" through the enforcement of university conduct
rules, and suppression of political dissent by government
agencies.

As the crisis in adjudication of campus misconduct
deepened, Cornell, ostensibly in the interest of fairness,
commissioned Sindler and others to reconstitute the student conduct code.[4] The Sindler Commission proudly
announced, "The University's primary objective should
not be law enforcement, which was the proper concern
of public authority." Rather, the university should "pro-

---

4 The "Sindler Commission," as it was called, made pioneering
   changes, according to Donald A. Downs, because it rejected the
   patronizing principle of *in loco parentis* which had governed the
   previous code.

tect the opportunity of all members of the Cornell community to pursue their educational goals effectively."[5]

The Commission's revisions, according to Donald A. Downs, author of a book about Cornell in 1969, were not considered "liberal" or "conservative." Nonetheless, Douglas Dowd, a left-wing economics professor, later criticized the judicial changes as unfair to students in political and racial cases. Others were annoyed at the lack of concrete guidelines. While the conflict between the judicial system and the anti-war movement had led to the establishment of the Sindler Commission, it provided abstract principles and changes in how violations were processed.[6] Yet, it did little or nothing to ameliorate the conflict itself. Cornell counsel Neil Stamp said: "This is one of the things that really disgusted me about the Sindler Commission. There were all these philosophic statements, but it didn't come down to something specific that would give us a road map."

Ironically, the Black Power movement intervened and kicked the Commission's innovations and its "rule of law" overboard. The time was ripe, and student activists ignored the Commission's abstractions. Resonating with civil-rights movements throughout the nation, the student-run African American Society (AAS) set off events culminating in the 1969 occupation of Willard Straight Hall. Demanding the creation of a black-studies program, the AAS became increasingly impatient as the work of the Committee responsible for a black-studies program dragged on. Several AAS members attended a black-power conference at Harvard and concluded that

---

5 Downs, op. cit., p. 67-8.

6 It is reminiscent of Tocqueville's comment about an American: "His ideas are all either extremely minute and clear, or extremely general and vague: what lies between is a void."

only an autonomous black college would meet their needs. Forty AAS members then raised this demand and refused to recognize the committee already charged with organizing a black-studies program. They formed a new committee consisting of themselves, and forcibly evicted personnel from the building slated to house the black-studies program. Subsequently, black students were cited for waving toy guns in the cafeteria and overturning vending machines, for conducting a sit-in at President Perkins's office, for running through the medical clinic, dancing on tables in the Straight's main dining room, and removing books from library shelves and dumping them at circulation desks. Some AAS students moved cushions from another building to the building assigned to house the black-studies program. The cushions were eventually returned and restitution was made for the cafeteria vandalism; nevertheless, the Cornell student Conduct Board cited the students for improper conduct.

After negotiating for days, President Perkins, who seemed to have the patience of Job, convinced the AAS that an autonomous black college was not possible.[7] Furthermore, by the time the Willard Straight incident occurred, only five student reprimands were being contested, due to the remarkable forbearance and patience of the university administration.

Toward the end of 1968, the AAS finally agreed to work with an administrative spokesman who headed a new committee on black studies. With the failure of the black college strategy, a moderate faction took command of the AAS, hoping to unite the black students behind a less confrontational posture. Still, while a blow-up was

---

7 A black student on one occasion grabbed Perkins by the collar during negotiations but this student and his companion were expelled for this assault from the AAS.

for the time being averted, the AAS continued to hold demonstrations for an autonomous black-studies program.[8]

In March 1969, the university judicial board affirmed the principles of the judicial system and stated its rationale for adjudicating the AAS students. Thereupon, five students were ordered to appear at a judicial hearing or face possible suspension; but they failed to appear.

White student protesters now complicated the scene. They disrupted on-campus recruiters for Chase Manhattan Bank to protest its dealings with South Africa. A special administration committee declined to charge these students and, although its decision was actually driven by faculty outrage toward the policy of apartheid in South Africa, the AAS denounced the committee's decision as racial favoritism toward whites.

The AAS denunciation was ignored, and the administration, at an emergency meeting, called for faculty support in the face of a breakdown of order. The faculty voted 306–229 to support the judicial board's citations of the five AAS members. Thereupon, 150 students appeared in place of the cited students before a student Conduct Board and protested its legitimacy. The Board announced that the suspensions of the cited students would be held "in abeyance" and asked the Faculty Committee on Student Conduct (FCSC), which reviewed cases decided by the Board, for assistance in reaching a final decision. The FCSC published a lengthy report supporting the Board that again asked the defendants to appear after the spring break. At this point, in a possibly unrelated occurrence, three white students were

---

8 Autonomy in this context seemed to mean greater student control over the selection of its Chair and the organization of the program.

assaulted on campus at night. Two identified their attackers as black. The third remembered nothing about the attack because he was beaten unconscious; he remained comatose for several days and suffered brain damage. The culprits were not identified and may not have been students.

A month later, Cornell Trustees voted to fund an Afro-American studies center in which students would have considerable decision-making power. Regardless, in that same month, the AAS published a statement presenting its case against the judicial system. The AAS student defendants were finally tried *in absentia* and the Conduct Board issued reprimands to three students. (The other two had left the university.) Shortly thereafter, false alarms broke out in dormitories. Within an hour a cross was burned in front of Waring House, the black women's residence. The relations between the AAS and university authorities had broken down, and the occupation of Willard Straight Hall followed.

During the evening of the occupation, Delta Upsilon fraternity members broke into the Straight from a side window, but were repelled. AAS allies outside then brought weapons into the building, transforming the occupation into a completely new ballgame.

Despite the AAS "resort to arms," thousands of Cornell students supported the black students. At a mass meeting, six thousand students raised their fists in response to a black leader, asking them who would support black students that night if they occupied Barlow Hall. However, other leaders informed the assembly that the faculty council had asked the Senate to hold an emergency meeting the next day to provide an opportunity to reverse the previous faculty approval of the reprimands against the black students. In light of this information, the student assembly decided to delay "moving in on the university" *en masse* led by the AAS. By delaying that move, they gave the faculty an opportunity to forestall dangerous consequences such as intervention by police and state troopers—and a riot in the Cornell ghetto.[9]

The following day, thousands of students stood outside the Arts quadrangle, awaiting the faculty decision. Some of the faculty who were against the student movement pointed to the pressure exerted by the students. They declared that if guns, and threats to occupy buildings, were used to force the faculty to reverse itself on matters affecting the judicial system, they might be used to similar ends on matters affecting academic freedom. Other faculty members, however, felt that academic freedom had nothing to do with nullifying the Conduct Board's reprimands. Professor Eldon Kentworthy, who specialized in Latin American politics and who witnessed events as they unfolded, cynically observed:

> There is certainly truth to the claim that tactics successful in one arena may be transferred to another, or that once the hiring and firing of teachers or the choice of course content area [is] decided by plebiscite, the university is finished. But weren't the students trapped in a guilt-by-anticipation? How did the faculty know they couldn't distinguish academic freedom issues from others? Was this, in fact, not a sophisticated put-down, a way of preserving faculty prerogatives on the whole range of issues in which academic freedom is not implicated or, if implicated, implicated in ways capable

---

9 According to black students' accounts.

of more than the faculty's interpretation?[10]

Students were angry, Kentworthy said, at the intrusion of the academic freedom issue into the faculty delibera- tions. To justify this intrusion, he observed, several polit- ical science and history professors claimed that they felt compelled to edit lectures or to avoid teaching certain subjects. However, these men seemed unable, according to Kentworthy, "to separate the essential conditions of academic freedom from the more nebulous conditions for good teaching from the still broader conditions for faculty comfort." Kentworthy, scornfully added,

> What we on the faculty failed to do, I believe, was make clear our preference for not having to act heroically, as well as to convince students that, given this preference, most of us are not effective teachers under heroic conditions. These personal and pedagogical needs, however, were swathed in the glowing rhetoric of academic freedom. 'Self-censorship' provided the link between the two. Consider, for example, this statement by Alan Sindler in a paper delivered to the American Political Science Association the fall following the crisis:

Kentworthy then quoted the following from Sindler's paper:

> When the environment for academic freedom is insufficiently supportive, as it

---

10 Eldon Kentworthy, "The Non-Militant Students." In (eds.) Cushing Strout and David I. Grossvogel, *Divided We Stand*. New York: Doubleday, 1970, pp. 75-89. See p. 86-9.

> recently has become at Cornell, the typical
> accommodation of a faculty man will be to
> play it safe, to teach students what they want
> to hear and will accept. Such faculty self-
> censorship undercuts academic freedom
> more pervasively and effectively than do the
> more dramatic incidents of disrupting
> classrooms, interrupting speakers, and the
> like.

Sindler's rationale was a coward's gambit, because it legitimated the intrusion of academic freedom into the faculty deliberations by appealing to cowardly sentiments.
Granted, the widespread self-censorship that accompa-
nies academic repression is appalling. And certainly, the
terrorist tactics employed by Jones and Garner—who assaulted Perkins and threatened Sindler and his colleagues with violent retribution—cannot in any setting
be condoned.[11] But appealing to cowardly sentiments to
defend academic freedom has an unpleasant odor, especially in the context in which this appeal was made.

For example, Kentworthy suggested that Sindler was-
n't truly addressing the situation at Cornell. Instead of
talking realistically about teaching conditions, he believed faculty members like Sindler

> ...either called up memories of the embattled
> leftist teachers of the McCarthy era or spun
> out images of some Newmanesque
> university that Cornell never was, at least
> not in the years I have known it. Forced to
> define the conditions for academic freedom,
> faculty members fell back on elaborate
> abstractions which translated as "whatever

---

11 Refer to the radio broadcast and threats.

makes the faculty man comfortable."

Kentworthy also noted that Sindler and others repeatedly resurrected an incident involving Professor McPhelin, which occurred a year before the sit-in at Straight Hall, to prove the existence of a "fateful trend" opposing academic freedom and leading to the April events. McPhelin had taught an introductory economics course and black students had accused him of making racist interpretations and remarks while referring to urban poor people and conditions accompanying poverty.[12] Also, when one of the black students questioned the relevance of a comparison of educational levels over time, McPhelin ignored the question.[13] After the class, the black students demanded and received an apology from McPhelin that was expressed publicly at the next session but they also prepared a formal rebuttal that was read aloud over McPhelin's objections.

Escalation of this issue, which included the demand for a black speaker who could present the "other side," led to the occupation, by about sixty mostly black students, of the Department of Economics office, and to negotiations with the administration for a black-studies program. When McPhelin resumed lecturing his topic after the sit-in, racial aspects of poverty—which had appeared in his original course outline—were omitted, ostensibly because he "was advised to stay off it."

The McPhelin incident was repeatedly used by

---

12 In a lecture on poverty, Professor McPhelin reportedly referred to social conditions in slums, including a passing characterization of children's games as "sick and perverse."

13 After the session, Prof. McPhelin promised to publicly apologize for not answering the question to the entire class the next meeting. But this did not end the matter.

Sindler and others to demonstrate the self-censorship accompanying the black students' threat to academic freedom as well as the "fateful trend" leading to the April events. But was this incident an appropriate example? Kentworthy didn't think it was; he noted that while faculty claimed the students had threatened McPhelin's freedom, they "failed to consider in that unhappy situation the academic freedom of McPhelin's students had been as much at issue as that of the professor."[14]

Indeed, a point can be made on the McPhelin incident by way of returning for just a moment to Berkeley and recalling teaching experiences at the School of Criminology. During the rise of the Black Power movement, black students challenged instructors whenever they sensed a racist comment—regardless whether they were right or not. On one occasion, a black student in one of Schwendinger's seminars furiously stalked out of the room but returned after Schwendinger ran after him and convinced him to calm himself, and to return and continue the debate. On another occasion, a black student and Schwendinger almost came to blows over their differences. But Schwendinger never believed these incidents ever threatened his freedom to speak his mind. He had obtained his bachelors toward the end of the Forties at The College of the City of New York, where students would rush to the library to get information to argue with their professors the next day. The Berkeley School had recaptured the vigorous interactions between students and teachers that made learning an extraordinary experience. In our opinion, McPhelin could have coura-

---

14 Kentworthy added, "Not unsurprisingly, the Williams poll discovered that 62% of the Cornell faculty defined academic freedom in terms applicable to the faculty alone, while only a fourth included a more than token student component in their definition."

geously affirmed his right to think as he pleased. He could have stood up for academic freedom, given the lecture as originally planned and engaged in a debate with the black students.

Certainly, the 6000 or 7000 students, who had raised their fists in support of the black students the night before the faculty vote on nullification was taken, did not believe Sindler's gambit was credible. They gave support because they sympathized with black students who had become fed up with other incidents: the burning cross placed in front of Waring House, a black women's campus residence;[15] the slow progress made toward the establishment of the black-studies program; and the Phi Delta Theta dance, which featured a black band but kept blacks out by requiring black students and blacks from the ghetto to pay while allowing whites to enter freely. When students compared these incidents with the so-called threat to academic freedom posed by the nullification of three minor penalties, Sindler's gambit lost all credibility.

As indicated, Kentworthy also viewed these events differently than Sindler. When Sindler and his crowd employed the coward's gambit, he wrote,

> Confronted with the faculty's inability either to talk convincingly about the real psychological conditions for effective teaching or to include in the abstract discussion of academic freedom recognition of student rights, many students came to view the whole issue as a red herring, as merely a part of the ideological

---

15 Analysis of the four feet by six feet cross found that it was composed of the same type of wood sold in the College arts supply store.

> superstructure faculty use to dismiss effective student pressure on any important issue. Representative of this view is a column [written by Mark Goldman] in the student newspaper, taking up this aspect of the April crisis from the perspective of ten months elapsed time.

After noting Goldman's column, Kentworthy states,

> Couched in classic liberal polemic, [Goldman's] arguments reaffirming the inviolability of academic freedom were attempts to defend and legitimize the power and position of the medieval oligarchs of the university—the faculty. Academic freedom ... represented an attempt to defend the concept of privilege, of class and to perpetuate a basically autocratic view of the world still endemic to much American thinking.[16]

The liberal rhetoric employed by Sindler touched on the final ambiguity of this affair. Sindler acclaimed, in the abstract, the rule of law and the principle of academic freedom. But were these abstractions compatible with his take on the Vietnam War or on racial inequality? What would he say if he were ordered to reconnoiter along Vietnamese trails trying hard not to step on our land mines or how would he justify killing a peasant who is encountered along the way? Would an ethical phase rule like "kill or be killed," that most egotistical justification, be enough to assuage his guilt in the act of gutting a peasant with a bayonet or blowing him away?

---

16 Mark Goldman, "On Academic Freedom," *Cornell Daily Sun*, February 20, 1970.

Where is Sindler as a human being who talks about moral absolutes and individual freedom when defending his position, but says nothing about the possibility of their negation when opposing values—such as being forced to face death or killing Vietnamese in an unjust war—outweigh his professed principles? The defense of Sindler's conduct at Cornell failed to depict him as a real human being whose invocation of abstract principles could never be taken at face value.

Donald A. Downs, in his book, *Cornell '69: Liberalism & the Crisis of the American University*, comfortably states, "The abandonment of liberal principles of freedom by the majority of liberals (for whatever reasons) was a powerful subplot of the Cornell story." In his scenario, "the chair of the Government Department, Allan Sindler, who became perhaps the most important faculty member in the entire yearlong affair" was among the small number of liberals who were willing to fight for academic freedom." Yet we know very little about Sindler's political attitudes. In Downs' account, he is a tintype, portrayed as a heroic one-dimensional man convinced about the sanctity of academic freedom. He appears to have no opinions that may moderate his belief in liberal absolutes. What about an equivocal commitment? Would he defend academic freedom if the quintessential bureaucrat, Adolph Eichmann, spoke about genocide at Cornell? How about Joseph Stalin? What about the ambassador to Vietnam, Averell Harriman? Should he be heard without protest when students who burned their draft cards were being forced to become cannon fodder in an imperialist war? In the formulaic scenario presented by scholars who have depicted events at Cornell, everything is unambiguous because their protagonists are never fleshed out and the relative weightings of contradictory ethical mandates that resolve moral conflicts in the real world, however changeable by circumstance, are not exposed.

Sindler, according to Downs, predicted that Cornell '69 "comprised a watershed event because of the introduction of firearms." It represented "the malaise of higher education, the declining self-confidence of academic men, the shattered consensus on academic values and the relation of the university to society, the bias of faculty in favor of the political Left, the conversion of white racial guilt and empathy to blacks to a quite different posture of abdicating judgment."[17] This list of indictments sounds so tragic a Homeric poet could have set it to verse. However, the real tragedy in Cornell's so-called "capitulation" to armed rebels involved the dismissal of the President, Perkins, whose unbelievable patience and gentle manner had led Cornell through an extraordinarily difficult time. He refused to expose the campus to the dangers of allowing law enforcement authorities to control student conduct on campus. In Berkeley, on the other hand, violent encounters with police in 1968–1969 were even greater than before.

BACK TO BERKELEY

While local police and state troopers were kept off the Cornell campus, nationally, in 1968-1969, police were used on nearly 100 campuses, the National Guard on six. More than 4,000 demonstrators were arrested. At Texas Southern University and in Orangeburg, South Carolina, black students were shot and killed. The National Guard occupied the black ghetto of Wilmington, Delaware, for nine months. Over a thousand Black Panther Party mem-

---

17 Downs, op. cit., p. 306.

bers were arrested in a nationally coordinated roundup. The two central events that year in Berkeley were the student strike led by the Third World Liberation Front (TWLF), spearheaded by the Asian students and the Black Student Union, which demanded the establishment of a Third World Studies department; and secondly, the destruction of People's Park. Massive retaliatory violence against demonstrators was employed in both of these events.

Rodney Stark, author of "Protest + Police = Riots," concluded from on-the-scene interviews and observations of the TWLF strike that police provoked the violence. His interviews indicate students were so enraged by the police brutality committed for years against students that any incident bringing "the pigs" on campus would produce massive demonstrations regardless of the reasons police were summoned. Whatever the issue, the angry students threw stones, bottles and cherry bombs or picked up gas grenades and tossed them back at police. Stark observed, "Time and again the police were used with very little reason, and time and again their arbitrary, massive and too often brutal performance spread and intensified the student discontent."

Stark illustrated this process with the strike called in January 1969 by the TWLF. Composed of non-white students, the TWLF struck to protest delays in the creation of a black studies program. In the following days, an ethnic studies program and an autonomous Third World College were added to the demands. Chancellor Heyns—like President Perkins at Cornell—met the TWLF part way, promising that the ethnic studies demand would receive positive action but he refused to speed up this process by altering normal committee procedures.

Reportedly, since the majority of Berkeley students felt the administration was accommodating to the TWLF (and the strikers excluded whites from their meetings), campus-wide support was minimal. At most, 300 persons were on the picket lines when the strike began. Campus routines were not disrupted; many students entered and left the campus without seeing a picket. Most students believed that the strike was primarily symbolic, merely showing solidarity with San Francisco State students who were still supporting the TWLF in a long, bitter strike against an implacable administration, headed by President Hayakawa.

During the night of the first day of the strike, the largest lecture room on campus, Wheeler Auditorium, was torched. TWLF leaders denounced the arson and denied all responsibility for it. Despite their anger, students were inclined to accept TWLF denials and put the blame on "crazies" among Telegraph Avenue "street people." Still, the strike suffered from the Wheeler Hall fire. The number of pickets dropped off and the strike was suspended for the weekend. It resumed on Monday; however, at this point, Stark exclaimed, "the incomprehensible occurred and a recurrent pattern was begun." The TWLF adopted a more militant tactic, refusing to allow students or faculty to pass through their picket line at Sather Gate. Technically, even though people could walk around the line rather than through it, this represented an obstruction of a public thoroughfare. So the picket line was declared illegal and off-campus police were summoned.

Summoning the police reinvigorated the strike. The following day, a thousand students marched around campus and joined the picket line. Summoned once again, the police dispersed the line. The next day, student support doubled. More than 2,000 students joined the line. Again, the police were called. Now, however, two black students were arrested, including a black student leader, Jim Nabors, who, according to the TWLF, was simply walking from class carrying his briefcase. According to Stark, this arrest "created an odor of police bigotry." (In the opinion of the authors of this study, it suggested that police were using information provided by the university administration or FBI to spot and arrest TWLF leaders.)[18]

In the following days, the students fought back with rocks and bottles. They overturned two police vans and hurled tear gas canisters back at the police who also used pepper foggers: buzzing machines emitting enormous clouds of gas. Even motorists on roads adjoining the campus were affected as they left their cars after being stopped by the gas and rioting. Students ran from the gas and the police but re-formed and demonstrated elsewhere on campus.

As the conflict went out of control, both strike leaders and the university tried to cool down the situation. Stark observed,

> But unlike the University of Chicago, the Berkeley administration was not able to take many risks to preserve campus peace. The Regents, led by Governor Reagan, an outspoken advocate of running campuses at 'the point of a bayonet,' had been for some time reducing the discretion of campus executive officers to deal with protest—a process which was further accelerated later in the course of the crisis. One presumes that

---

18 On another day, Nabors was again singled out, pinned to a bench and viciously beaten by several policemen.

> Chancellor Heyns was under terrific
> pressure to get tough and to use the police.
> To make matters worse, Heyns had no
> authority over outside police. He only had
> the power to decide whether to call them for
> aid in a given situation, but once called they
> were completely independent. As one
> campus official put it, 'we have only the
> power of persuasion over the police, but
> they're not in much mood to be persuaded.'

Differing from The University of Chicago and Cornell, Berkeley was a public institution where the Governor could initiate police intervention. Even though the university administration and TWLF leaders tried to cool things down and the campus had become peaceful without a police presence, Stark reported: "Alameda County Sheriff Frank Madigan publicly released a letter to Governor Reagan, in which he threatened to refuse to continue furnishing police to the campus unless he was given a free hand to crack down." Madigan alleged the university had refused to take action against violators and called for the declaration of a "State of Extreme Emergency." Reagan responded by declaring an emergency and activating the National Guard.

The People's Park Protests

The second attempt to suppress massive protests in 1968–1969 involved both students and Bay Area residents who responded to the brutal attack on the "People's Park" demonstration. A large partly unpaved and much neglected lot used for parking a few blocks south of main campus—just off Telegraph Avenue had been taken over by "street people" and radicals. These people graded the lot, planted a vegetable garden and erected a children's playground from donated materials. The lot was used by residents in the area but street people passing through Berkeley often slept there. Because of this public use, the park was called "People's Park" even though it was university property.

Although South campus residents sorely needed a park, neither the Berkeley City Council nor the university administration had been receptive to park proposals from citizens and the College of Environmental Design. When People's Park was constructed, however, the university administration, despite public criticism and after neglecting the lot, suddenly announced it had obtained funds to construct a soccer field there. Although everyone knew this plan was a ruse to reassert university control, attempts were made to negotiate the issue, but the negotiations collapsed.[19]

After the perimeter of the lot was bulldozed, several thousand students, faculty and community residents left a noon protest rally and marched down Telegraph Avenue toward the lot. But they never reached their destination. Police armed with gas, clubs, rifles and pistols attacked them. An historian, W. J. Rorabaugh reports, "*The San Francisco Chronicle* published a photograph of one demonstrator being shot in the back while fleeing down a side street." Officers for some unexplained reason released gas on campus; in fact, some officers threw gas into Tolman Hall, the School of Education building, and held the doors shut to prevent people from escaping. More than 100 people in the demonstration were shot with birdshot, buckshot, and rock salt fired from police shotguns. No protester fired at the police. Yet the police

19 Depending on the "spin" required, university public relations said the lot was slated to become a soccer field, student dorms or parking lot. Eventually, it was turned into a parking lot.

killed one man and blinded another.[20] An officer, pulled from a burning vehicle, was almost killed by the enraged crowd.

For more than a week, tens of thousands of people from the San Francisco Bay Area reacted to this event with massive demonstrations. Governor Reagan called out the National Guard. Berkeley was occupied for almost two weeks by 2700 Guardsmen and thousands of police. During this military siege, the Governor suspended constitutional rights. A bright undergraduate, Steve Wasserman, in a monograph entitled *History of the School of Criminology: From 1915 to the Present*, avowed, "A reign of terror, with heavily armed police tear gassing and smashing into homes and dormitories hit Berkeley and especially the student community with a vengeance."[21]

The siege, hundreds injured, one person killed and another blinded, and almost one thousand arrests galvanized moderates and radicals at the university. "Meanwhile over three hundred faculty members including Nobel laureates signed a petition pledging not to teach while the city was under military occupation[22] and some

---

20 A member of the School of Criminology's Advisory Council, Alameda County District Attorney Frank Coakley, declared that his office would make a "complete and thorough investigation" of events in Berkeley and that "appropriate action" would be taken "as has been done in other episodes of mass violence and criminality," according to Steve Wasserman, *History of the School of Criminology: From 1915 to the Present*. May 1973, unpublished monograph, p. 49.

21 Ibid.

22 *The Daily Californian*, "Faculty Members Won't Teach" Wednesday, May21, 1969 contains the original call for faculty signatures and demonstrations against police on other UC campuses.

verbally confronted Reagan in his office in Sacramento. Statewide actions of solidarity with Berkeley involved thousands of students in San Diego, Riverside, Los Angeles, Santa Cruz, San Jose, and Stanford. Faced with a statewide crisis, and an outraged outburst from liberals influential in the state (some of whose children, while on a picnic near the campus, had been inadvertently gassed by the National Guard), Reagan was forced to lift the citywide curfew and withdraw most of his troops."[23]

Faculty and other employees in the School of Education, Sociology Department and other departments condemned the UCB administration and Sheriff Madigan. Labor organizations including AFT locals 1470 (faculty) and 1570 (graduate teaching assistants), Alameda County Central Labor Council, and American Federation of State Council and Municipal Employees (AFSCME) joined the condemnation. Student associations, World Peace Committee of the Unitarian Church, Unitarian Lutheran Chapel, over 130 civil service employees largely at the county level, Committee of Concerned Asia Scholars, and other organizations added their voices. They asked the university administration to parley once again with The People's Park Negotiating Committee for a reasonable solution, such as that proposed by the College of Environmental Design.[24] But the university dug in its heels and stood its ground.

Still, the university's right to determine the fate of the park had been challenged. A poster, *Who Owns the Park?*, exclaimed, "Someday a petty official will appear with a piece of paper which states that the University of California owns the land of the People's Park. Where did

---

23 Wasserman, op. cit. p. 49.

24 The College recommended a representative body would control the use of the park.

that piece of paper come from? What is it worth?" The poster answered these questions. It said,

> A long time ago the Costanoan Indians lived in the area now called Berkeley. They had no concept of land ownership. They believed that the land was under the care and guardianship of the people who used it and lived on it. Then the Catholic missionaries took the land away from the Indians. The Mexican Government took the land away from the Church. The Americans beat the Mexicans and forced them to sign away their property. The US government then sold the land to white settlers and gave them a land title in exchange for money. While there were still some Indians who claimed the land, the American army killed them. Finally, some very rich men, who run the University of California, bought the land and, after a boarding house that had been built on the land was destroyed, it became a parking lot.

The poster declared:

> We are building a park on the land. We will take care of it and guard it, in the spirit of the Costanoan Indians. When the University comes with its land title we will tell them: 'Your land title is covered in blood. We won't touch it. Your people ripped off the land from the Indians a long time ago. If you want it back now, you will have to fight for it again.'

PROTESTING THE CAMBODIAN INVASION

The people symbolized by this poster lost the fight for People's Park. Still, even their defeat did not stop further protests. In 1970, after the Cambodian invasion showed President Nixon and Henry Kissinger had lied about deescalating the war, the demonstrations started up again. As millions of people throughout the country took to the streets, thousands of Berkeley students called for an immediate end to the war, the cessation of war-related university research and the release of imprisoned dissidents, including Black Panther Party leader Bobby Seale.

The Cambodian invasion provoked the greatest crisis in the history of the university. Over 2000 activists met on campus, elected a strike committee that formed "action groups" to campaign for the cancellation of classes and their replacement with "reconstituted" student-run classes, supporting opposition to the war and "democratizing" the university.[25] This "reconstitution," as Wasserman observes, "represented the climax of nearly a decade of student struggle in terms of the scope and quality of student initiative, collectivity and social consciousness."[26]

An unprecedented number of faculty joined students protesting the war. Despite threats from Governor Reagan and administration, the great majority of the UCB faculty, in an emergency Academic Senate meeting,

---

25 A national strike and informational center was established at Brandeis University. On May 11th, over 500 students attended a National Student Strike Conference in San Jose, California. On virtually every campus, a strike coordinating committee was spontaneously formed and linked up with the newly created national center.

26 Wasserman, op. cit., p. 53.

passed a resolution on May 4th calling for the university-wide cessation of classes. The next day, the Criminology Students Association (CSA) voted unanimously to back a general strike and asked the School faculty to suspend academic activity in accordance with the Senate resolution. Voting 15 to 2 in favor of the strike, the Criminology faculty overwhelmingly assented.[27]

After a meeting attended by 17,000 students in the Greek Theater approved the "reconstitution" of the university, Governor Reagan suddenly broke his 16-month-old promise to keep the University of California open "at the points of bayonets" if necessary. He ordered all colleges and universities in California to be closed down. Yet, despite his order, thousands of students swarmed on campus to hold teach-ins, rallies and organizing sessions devoted to ending the war and to curbing the bureaucratic organization of the university.

The student movement met with partial success. Not surprisingly, the attempt to reconstitute the bureaucracy failed. Still, the seemingly endless leaflet writing, teach-ins and agitation among students reinforced popular outrage occurring throughout the country. It amplified the popular outrage that forced Nixon, three months after the invasion, to withdraw US troops from Cambodia. The invasion had turned into a military and political catastrophe.

---

27 Diamond, according to Wasserman (p. 52-53), on June 2nd reported "There is considerable pressure on the administration from . . . higher levels of administration regarding the current situation on campus. It is expected that some punitive measures will be taken by the state which would effect whole segments of the University population (such as all faculty)." Diamond went on to say that individuals who failed in all or part of their professional duties would be financially penalized.

The military withdrawal, however, did not turn the clock back and remove the harms done to student protestors.

> At Kent State 4 students were shot and killed, and 10 were wounded by gunfire; at Jackson State 2 students were shot and killed and 12 wounded. In Augusta Georgia 6 black students were killed and the police and National Guard wounded 20, while at the University of New Mexico 11 students were bayoneted. Altogether, during the movement's highpoint in May of 1970, over 100 people were killed or seriously wounded by police or National Guardsmen and more than 2000 people were arrested for political reasons in the first two weeks of May alone. A demonstration called by the anti war New Mobilization Committee brought out over 100 000 people to the nations capital in a weeks notice, only to be faced with over 25 000 police and soldiers armed with live ammunition.[28]

Among college and university students, the never-ending strikes, demonstrations and occupations of buildings created an historically unprecedented crisis of legitimation. On June 15th, 1970, the *New York Times* reported that 42 percent of all students believed the American Constitution needed major changes. As early as 1968, the pollster Daniel Yankelovich reported that at least 368 000 people strongly agreed on the need of a "mass revolutionary party" in the US and that after the student strike of 1970, over a million students considered themselves to be

---

28 For this list of atrocities, found in "The Fire Last Time" by Tom Keefer in *the Peak, U. of Guelph's Alternative Student Newspaper.*

"revolutionaries." In early 1971 the *New York Times* discovered that four out of ten students (more than 3 million people) thought that a revolution was needed in the United States.[29]

COMMUNITY CONTROL OF POLICE

Confrontations between anti-war protesters and police continued into 1971 when Bowker was selected as Chancellor to replace Heyns who resigned because Reagan and the Regents' repeatedly attacked him for not being tough enough at coping with the students.

But the confrontations were not merely expressed in violent encounters. In fact, to stop the cycle of violence in Berkeley, some radicals at the School of Criminology began to work with the Black Panther Party and Ron Dellums, the black Congressman who represented Alameda County, at finding peaceful solutions. This attempt, however, only deepened the antagonism between the radicals at the School and the police.

As indicated, police had repeatedly attacked UCB protesters with fists, kicks, clubs, cattle prods, tear gas, pepper foggers, pistols and shotguns. From the FSM movement onward, Berkeley students were enraged whenever "the pigs" entered the campus. In addition, every major black protest movement in Berkeley and Oakland experienced repeated police provocation. In many black communities, they were regarded as an army of occupation.

Yet, efforts to reform the police failed. Citizen police-review boards were rendered powerless. Major recommendations for police reform produced by national and

---

29 Ibid.

state commissions were never implemented.[30] Racial integration of police departments materialized at a snail's pace while federal funds were poured into riot control, fire power and communications equipment. The police remained an ultra-conservative political force.

In 1971, over 15,000 Berkeley citizens petitioned the City to place a "Community Control of Police Amendment" before voters in City elections. Work on this amendment had been initiated by the Black Panther Party but radicals at the School helped formulate it in an attempt to decentralize the police department and to place power in the hands of grass-roots councils. City officials reacted hysterically and the city attorney deceitfully branded the Amendment "unconstitutional" even though the State Constitution gave citizens the right to alter city charters through referendums. The city manager threatened to resign if the Amendment passed and the ultra-conservative *Berkeley Daily Gazette*, repeatedly carried headlines warning that if the radicals were successful, they would destroy Berkeley's fabric of life.

The Berkeley Police Department, ninety of whose officers had signed a petition calling for a "crack-down" on radicals, misused public funds and time to agitate against the Amendment at meetings throughout the city. This opposition reflected the reality described by Joseph Lohman before he died. He wrote: "The police function [is] to support and enforce the interests of the dominant political, social and economic interests of the town, and only incidentally to enforce the law."[31]

Within the School, the amendment was hotly debated. On January 14, 1971 the Criminology Students Associa-

---

30 Kerner, Walker, and Scranton
31 Quoted in A. Niederhoffer, *Behind the Badge*, p.12.

tion (CSA) became the first student organization to endorse the measure. It passed a resolution recognizing "the urgent need for new alternatives to the present institutional structures of law enforcement, and the need for the development of more responsive community oriented police programs."

By March, some faculty, including Platt, Takagi and Schwendinger, publicly asked Berkeley citizens to back the Amendment.[32] They stated,

> As criminologists at the University of California and citizens who work in Berkeley concerned about creating a police department which respects and acts upon democratic principles of government, we urge your support of this amendment . . . For citizens, it will provide participation in the governance of an important public institution, fair and independent grievance procedures and more efficient protection of the public from serious crimes: For the police, it will mean community respect and support as well as a truly professional role which emphasizes a commitment to legality. And finally, it will help to transform policing from a quasi-military role of repression to one which encourages equal protection under the law and conflict resolution. Community control offers an opportunity to minimize police illegality and to fully protect constitutional rights of free speech, assembly and political expression.

Platt supported the Amendment in a letter to the *San*

---

32 Others signing the statement included Menachim Amir, Nathan Adler, Vonnie Gurgin and Richard Korn.

Francisco Chronicle, August 25, 1970. He wrote:

> The proposed initiative . . . is aimed at
> making government representative and
> democratic. The police are an important and
> powerful institution; they are supposed to be
> 'public servants.' The initiative seeks to
> restore popular and civilian government of
> the police . . . The initiative is also supported
> in theory by a considerable body of
> criminological literature urging civilian
> controls of the police. The initiative is a
> thoughtful proposal, based on careful study
> and consultation with community groups. It
> seeks much needed democratic change
> through the electoral process.

The Chronicle responded immediately to Platt's letter
with an August 27th editorial disingenuously and demagogically proclaiming its astonishment that "a criminologist, of all people, would advocate what amounts to
ghettoization of the police and the abandonment of the
many pioneering programs for better race relations for
which Berkeley has taken pride."

Of the faculty who signed the endorsement, only one
person, Paul Takagi, had tenure. Furthermore, on March
7, 1971, Takagi, in a separate statement entitled "Technocrats vs. Public Servants," clarified his endorsement.
Identified as the Associate Dean of the School of Criminology, a former deputy probation officer in Alameda
County, a former state parole officer in Los Angeles and
a correctional classification officer in San Quentin
Prison, he stated,

> The social problems in this community are

so serious that I feel the Charter amendment addresses itself to the question of whether bureaucratic elites and technocrats and political officials who, for the most part, serve special economic and political interest groups should continue to govern the affairs of the people in the community. Shall we have that kind of government, or should the people in the community begin to play a larger role in determining how the agencies should meet the needs of the people?

The genius of this proposal is that it does recognize that conflicts exist within a community. Instead of trying to deal with these conflicts on the basis of threat of penalty or coercion, it begins to recognize that differences do exist and that conflicts do emerge, and rather than attempting to bludgeon people into conformity, it provides for an opportunity to explore the source of these conflicts and then to begin to attack the problem.

Because the acceptance of this legislative proposal meant the decentralization of the police and placing them under direct control of community residents, the police reacted swiftly. In the closing hours of the campaign, Wasserman observed, O. W. Wilson, who was once Dean of the School, unheard from in years and living in retirement in San Diego, sent a telegram repudiating community control of the police. The telegram published in the April 5, 1971 edition of the *Daily Californian* in the form of a capitalized advertisement sponsored by the "One Berkeley Community," an organization formed to defeat the radical police proposal read:

THE CHARTER PROPOSAL FOR
'COMMUNITY CONTROL OF POLICE'
COULD DESTROY THE BERKELEY
POLICE DEPARTMENT, A FINE AND
FAIR ORGANIZATION OF MEN AND
WOMEN REPRESENTING CITIZENS
OF AN AMERICAN COMMUNITY

PROPONENTS OF THE
ILL-CONCEIVED MEASURE INCLUDE
SEVERAL NON-TENURE FACULTY
MEMBERS OF THE SCHOOL OF
CRIMINOLOGY WHO ARE NOT
QUALIFIED TO SPEAK FOR THEIR
COLLEAGUES NOR THE UNIVERSITY
OF CALIFORNIA

I URGE MY ACADEMIC ASSOCIATES
AND FELLOW CALIFORNIANS TO
VOTE NO TO DECISIVELY DEFEAT
CHARTER AMENDMENT ONE IN THE
APRIL ELECTIONS

O. W. WILSON, DEAN EMERITUS,
SCHOOL OF CRIMINOLOGY

The majority of registered voters voted against the Amendment. Platt, who was a leader in the struggle for community control, became a target. The university administration had the pretext it needed to punish Platt for his participation in democratic politics. The University police, as we will see in Chapter 7, were used as the instrument of retribution.

For understanding this phase in the School's history, the radical effort to formulate model legislation and fight for its adoption in a democratic election is important. The so-called "radical impossibilism" cited by Geis, in this case, involved an attempt to work within the system and stop the police brutality and cycles of violence that overwhelmed students and citizens in the San Francisco Bay Area.

Ironically, neither the police nor the National Guard ever stopped the demonstrations at the University in Berkeley. The violence over the TWLF demands ended when university concessions were in place. And the violence between police and the anti-war movement ended when the Vietnam War ended. These elemental facts, however, are conveniently ignored by academic hacks who have blamed the "usual suspects" when explaining why the School was closed.

5 | The Counter-Reformists

L et's start with a comparison from two disparate moments in history. There are parallels between the anti-reformist campaign against the School of Criminology radicals in Berkeley and the counter-reformation led by 16th-century Jesuit scholars at Collegio Romano, in Rome. The scholars campaigned against scientists who, they believed, undermined their dogmatic interpretation of biblical events. Working covertly at first, they gradually mounted a campaign that convicted Galileo Galilei as a heretic and, for all practical purposes, put him in solitary confinement by sentencing him to a lifetime of house arrest.[1] More recently, and closer to home, around 1971, a counter-reformist faculty network at Berkeley worked covertly with the university administration and state government to repress the "heretics" in the School of Criminology. Eventually, they succeeded in exiling the radicals and destroying the School the radicals had helped create.

This repression was duplicated across the country. Michael Miles reported in 1972 that as "student unrest" dropped off nationally, university authorities carried out

---

1   Pietro Redondi, 1987. *Galileo Heretic.* (trans., Raymond Rosenthal) Princeton, NJ: Princeton University Press, p. 135.

"more firm action" against the student movement than at any other time. These authorities had learned from bitter experience in the late 1960s that "direct engagement involving the use of police force, summary dismissals and the like did what the radical issues of imperialism and racism by themselves could not: they mobilized a majority of students and a significant minority of the faculty to the radicals' defense." Their new repressive strategy therefore recommended avoiding the radicalizing effect produced by police crackdowns. It urged the patient and careful choice of the "right moments" to remove the "hard core" students and faculty who supposedly had "manipulated" the "concerned masses."[2] While the "hard core" was being removed, the authorities would accommodate to movement demands, making moderate reforms that would co-opt the remaining dissenters.

Such counter-reformist alliances at Berkeley usually relied on networks that formed and reformed depending upon circumstances. In 1969, for instance, a group called The Council for an Academic Community (CAC) appears to have been established during or after the Third World Strike to "work informally toward the preservation of rational discourse in the face of violent and coercive confrontation."[3] In 1970, the CAC had 29 members and most, like Paul Seabury, a public policy professor targeted by the anti-war movement,[4] Melvin

---

2 Miles, Michael. 1972-73. "The Triumph of Reaction." *Change: The Magazine of Higher Learning* 30-36 (Winter) p. 30.

3 The date of its formation and its subsequent 1970 "statement of purpose," entitled "CAC Principles," was obtained from the UCB Bancroft Library archives. (The faculty club may have required a note about CAC's aims to provide a meeting room in 1969 and the right to use the club's name on the 'letterhead' of declarations issued in 1970.)

4 Seabury was a former member of the President's Foreign

Webber, who taught naval architecture, and Charles To-
bias from Engineering and Lawrence Radiation Laboratory, a research center linked with the war machine, were
not administrators or aspiring administrators. However,
some like Robert Scalapino during the free-speech crisis
had been the Political Science Department Chairman.
George Maslach, as Provost, monitored undergraduate
enrollment in the School of Criminology during its final
years. Earl Cheit had been an Executive Vice Chancellor[5] while others, such as Martin Trow functioned, in the
1960s and 1970s, as directors of research centers. Alan
P. Sindler, who has been introduced previously, joined
the CAC shortly after he quit Cornell. At Berkeley, he
was employed as a public policy professor but, in later
years, became Dean of the Graduate School of Public
Policy.

Still another member, Lincoln Constance, had been a
Department Chairman, Dean and Academic Vice Chan-
cellor. During the free speech conflict, he represented
the Chancellor's office to the faculty. In an interview,
Constance confessed when he first met with Mario
Savio,

Intelligence Advisory Board. He was, among other things, a
member of the board of directors of the Committee on the Present
Danger, a militantly anti-Soviet pro-defense lobby of which
President Reagan was formerly a member. He edited "The
Grenada Papers" for the Institute for Contemporary Studies, a
group founded by Edwin Meese. (See Richard Hatch and Sara
Diamond, "The World Without War Council," *Covert Action
Information Bulletin*, #31, Winter 1989. Also, #45. Sara Diamond,
"Shepherding," *Covert Action Information Bulletin*, #27, Spring
1987.)

5 Cheit in later years became Dean of the School of Business. He
also became a Senior Advisor to the Asia Foundation, which had
been a CIA conduit. In the 1990s Scalapino was honored at Asia
Foundation and Kissinger was member of the award committee.

> I had to control myself because I wanted to
> reach across the table and smack Savio right
> in the face because he was insolent and
> brash, and frankly I thought he was off his
> rocker. . . . I'd have loved to punch him in
> the nose, and I think it might have been an
> historical favor if I had.[6]

As the prior chapter indicated, a number of faculty had responded to the 1970 Cambodian invasion by refusing to teach. (Also, Governor Reagan was actually forced to shut down the university temporarily.) When classes resumed, some of these faculty members, depending on their courses and expertise, devoted classroom time to ethical, legal, social, economic or political factors affecting the course of the War. Since the invasion further exposed the criminal policies behind the War, radical faculty at the School felt obligated to devote classroom sessions to such topics as war crimes and crimes against humanity.

But such faculty responses to the Cambodian invasion galvanized the counter-reformists. In 1969 the CAC had intended to achieve its aims unofficially. A year later, however, the faculty response to the invasion brought it out of the closet. The CAC informed the UCB faculty that while the university provides room for intellectual dissent it should remain free of political advocacy and action. Academic freedom, the CAC added, depends

---

6 Lincoln Constance "Versatile Berkeley Botanist: Plant Taxonomy and University Governance." Interviewed by Ann Lage in 1986. Regional Oral History Office, The [University of California, Berkeley] Bancroft Library, 1987. These remarks are in the section incredibly entitled, "Chancellor Strong: Liberal, Contemplative, Principled." (This information was obtained from Web pages of UCB's oral history documents, which are not numbered.)

upon "the rejection of all efforts to politicize the University, and especially to transform it into a political weapon." Even though "the faculty alone" has the right to decide what happens in the classroom, the content of their courses must not be compromised by political aims.[7]

"After U.S. intervention in Cambodia in May 1970," CAC continued, "many classes were dismissed and some were interrupted by dissidents seeking to coerce professors and students, who wanted to carry on academic pursuits, into quitting." To support faculty and students who rejected efforts to politicize the university and transform it into a political weapon, the CAC announced that it took a full-page advertisement in the *Daily Californian* and nearly 500 signatures were received showing agreement with its principles. The CAC expressed its intention to resist attempts to politicize the university perpetrated by "members of the university" (i.e., students and faculty) as well as public officials and people at large. It concluded,

> To protect the foundations of this University, open membership in CAC is now proposed. If academic responsibility is not taken by faculty now it will be assumed by forces outside the University. A larger organization is planned and duly elected officers will take over for the calendar year 1971. Membership is free and all members of Academic senate are invited to join.

---

7 Council for an Academic Community. 1969-1970. "CAC Principles & Statement of Purpose." UCB Bancroft Library archives. This document appears to have been issued during the 1970 fall semester.

The CAC's late 1970 campaign was in part aimed at closing a breach opened by the faculty trade union, Local 1474 of the American Federation of Teachers (AFT). During the summer of 1970, thousands of students left Berkeley and support for anti-war protests was scaled down. But the Chancellor's office took advantage of this circumstance to harass faculty members concerning alleged "excesses" generated by the anti-war protests. For example, in August 1970, Professor of Mathematics Morris W. Hirsch was reprimanded and docked a week's pay. But a memo issued by Local 1474 asserted that the most elementary forms of due process were violated in Professor Hirsch's case and that the Chancellor's evidence appeared to be either irrelevant or insubstantial. Local 1474 backed Hirsch's appeal to the Senate's Committee on Privilege and Tenure and called upon faculty to inform the Union immediately if they received calls to discuss teaching with Vice Chancellor Connick. To forestall additional administrative actions, Local 1474 asked support for the AFT's efforts to incorporate the existing disciplinary powers of the Administration into a contract between the Regents and the faculty, to be negotiated through collective bargaining.

During the 1970 fall semester, however, the restored administration-faculty alliance finally recovered control of the Academic Senate, which had been lost five years earlier in the debate about the FSM. The alliance, of course, was not interested in negotiations that would help protect opposition professors like Hirsch. Instead, it moved aggressively to toughen the disciplinary rules in order to shield its own members and to curb the anti-war movement.

But its reliance on the Academic Senate rather than AFT collective bargaining meant traversing the Byzantine corridors of faculty self-governance. To a degree, the faculty policed itself and this policing was channeled through the Senate and its committees. Consequently, to neutralize, threaten or punish the opposition faculty, the CAC had to manipulate the Senate and stack the committees.

Also, a successful campaign was not assured just by Machiavellian politics on a local level. It required similar efforts by administrative-faculty alliances on all 9 campuses of the University of California system, because the Assembly of the Academic Senate, composed of delegates from each one of these campuses, was charged with the task of incorporating revisions into a single code for the entire system.[8]

In November 1970, in Berkeley, the Senate Policy Committee opened the door to local recommendations for changes in the code. It got the Senate to approve a resolution asking the Academic Freedom and Policy Committees to jointly prepare a statement on professional conduct and faculty discipline. The Privilege and Tenure Committee was also asked to add its opinion especially regarding disciplinary procedures.

On January 11, 1971, the three committees—Senate Policy, Academic Freedom and Privilege and Tenure—reported back to the Senate, submitting a draft of their revisions to the code.[9] The joint report submitted on January 11 said the Committees were "mindful" of the necessity to formulate "broad outlines of punishable

---

8 The 9 UC campuses were at Berkeley, Davis, Irvine, Los Angeles, Riverside, San Diego, San Francisco, Santa Barbara and Santa Cruz.

9 The final draft is in the joint reports of the Committees to the Academic Senate circulated on February 4 and presented for approval at the February 16th Senate meeting.

misconduct" rather than a "detailed criminal code."[10] Apparently, the new rules were designed to cover all possible contingencies created by faculty that, in the Committee's view, "significantly impaired the University's particular interests as an institution of higher learning."

On June 29, 1971, the statewide Assembly of the Academic Senate adopted a revised faculty conduct code for the 9 University of California campuses.[11] The justifications for the revisions crammed with platitudes, invoked supposedly "mutually supportive relationships" between academic freedom and the mission of the university. Embedded in its decorous verbiage were prohibitions against faculty intrusion of material unrelated to their courses, their failure to meet class, their participation in disruptions or interference in the classrooms, their unauthorized use of University resources or facilities for political purposes, their intentional disruption of functions or activities authorized by the University, their intentional disobedience of University rules and incitement of others to disobey these rules, especially "when such incitement constitutes a clear and present danger that violence against persons or property will occur."

Disciplinary consequences were coupled with these prohibitions. Violations could be punished by censure; docking of pay; deferral of an impending promotion or

---

10 The Senate Policy Committee in November 1970 had objected to the administration's plans to adopt the criminal code as a model by preparing a "precise delineation" of punishable faculty offenses. Employing this model for revising the code, in its view, would be "insufficiently inclusive" as well as "rigid."

11 University Bulletin. 1971, June 28. "The Faculty Code of Conduct as Approved By the Assembly of the Academic Senate." in *University Bulletin: A Weekly Bulletin for the Staff of the University of California.*

merit increase; suspension without pay; demotion in professorial rank or in salary; and dismissal from the employ of the University. While enforcement of these prohibitions required judicial procedures administered by faculty committees, the Chancellor was permitted to impose an interim suspension, with full pay, on a faculty member, without following these procedures when he deemed it probable that keeping a faculty member on the job would be harmful to the University community.

Some of these prohibitions and punishments in-themselves seem reasonable—including the rule against incitement of violence even though no faculty member had ever been accused of such incitement and even though this rule ignored the fact that the criminal law prohibited such incitement. Nevertheless, when faculty opposition to the Cambodian crisis is kept in mind, the political conformity that could be served by this conduct code seems ominous.

In February 1971, a month after the three committees had submitted their joint report, the Berkeley Senate was confronted with a request to expand the mission of the Academic Freedom Committee. Carefully orchestrated speeches, memos and bulletins about "alarming threats" to academic freedom were being circulated during the time of this request. The CAC, for instance, had issued a bulletin, entitled "THE INTERNAL THREATS TO ACADEMIC FREEDOM." It urged the Committee to gather information about the sources of these threats that could hold opposition faculty liable for violating the code of conduct. This bulletin observed,

> Berkeley has experienced a series of serious
> internal attacks on academic freedom: the
> so-called 'War Crimes Commission,' the

threats and attacks against Profs. Glaser, Jensen, Scalapino, Searle, Teller, and others, and the recent efforts to disrupt Profs. Jensen's and Scalapino's classes. These actions are part of a pattern of efforts to coerce and intimidate faculty members, to punish them for their views, and to serve as a warning to others who might hold or express similar views. These are attacks on the intellectual and academic freedom of our colleagues by self-appointed censors in the community, in the student body, or on the faculty.[12]

The CAC did not identify the culprits among the faculty. In fact, it granted, "some members of the faculty have felt that we should take no notice of these attacks on our colleagues." However, it claimed,

. . . our silence in the face of these attacks would lead to a gradual callousing of our sensibilities, and a readiness to accept as 'normal' actions that only a little earlier would have provoked shocked condemnation. Already there are signs that we are accommodating ourselves to a situation in which faculty members can associate themselves with groups such as the 'War Crimes Commission' whose avowed intention is to intimidate colleagues (our emphasis).

---

12 The February 1971 bulletin is entitled, "THE INTERNAL THREATS TO ACADEMIC FREEDOM." The bulletin heading also contains these words: "Faculty Center: Occasional notes from the Council for an Academic Community, Published six or more times a year by CAC at Berkeley, Calif."

Adding that these attacks on highly visible teachers exerted "a subtle pressure on others who teach in sensitive areas," the CAC urged the Academic Senate Committee on Academic Freedom to investigate reported violations without waiting, as has been its practice, for a request from an "aggrieved" faculty member.[13]

Importantly, a few days later, a speech by Chancellor Heyns on academic freedom was printed in *Campus Report*, published by the UCB Office of Public Information on February 19, 1971. Heyns thought the Academic Freedom Committee should make a "searching study" of instances in which the freedoms of faculty and students have been "interfered with." The Chancellor asserted, "The stand that it takes will have a major impact on the quality of academic life here." But, curiously, the Academic Freedom Committee's stand and the results of the study were already widely known by the faculty before Heyns made his speech. They had been expressed in a formal statement circulated on February 8, which like the CAC bulletin was subtitled, "Internal Threats to Academic Freedom."[14] Because Sindler, too, was a member of the Academic Freedom Committee, his name appeared at the end of the statement below that of the Committee Chairman, who also was a Chairman of a Law School Department.

The Committee statement described the following "threats" to freedom. It reported that "several faculty

---

13 In addition, the bulletin condemned "efforts at coercion or intimidation of faculty members or students, from whatever source" and announced the university administration and Senate's Committee on Academic Freedom were undertaking "a broader inquiry into this whole problem."

14 Academic Freedom Committee, February 8, 1971, "A Statement of the Committee on Academic Freedom: Internal Threats to Academic Freedom." Academic Senate, Berkeley Division.

members and administrators had been the object of investigation by a self-appointed 'war crimes tribunal'." Students and non-students had even marched to the home of one professor denouncing him as a war criminal, but the police had turned them back. An anonymous handbill distributed at the edge of campus listed another professor's address, sketched a map pinpointing his residence and urged readers to challenge his actions by calling his residence to discuss matters with him. Still another professor, the statement said, had been called a racist and made the subject of a campaign aimed at exposing his "controversial" research findings and published opinions. Research institutes, it said, had also been targeted because their work was "objectionable to some persons." A prominent guest speaker had cancelled his lecture out of fear, and others had been subjected to heckling and ridicule.

The Committee appeared deeply troubled. It said "every person," engaged in "similarly controversial research or whose ideas may be abhorrent to some," was being threatened by this harassment. It also frighteningly declared, "The victims of campus vigilante activities include not only those who are identified publicly as targets or symbols but many who may fear that they too will become objects of future attacks." This fear, the Committee alleged, reached beyond the handful of faculty being harassed. "It matters not that the ultimate threat may be averted—that the classroom may not actually be disrupted, the lecture stopped, the house burned or the laboratory bombed; the hazard to academic freedom adheres in a climate of fear that may be caused by such forces," the Committee concluded.

The Committee finally requested "cooperation" from the faculty while inquiring into all of these threats to

academic freedom. But what, precisely, did "cooperation" really mean? Joining the network of counter-reformists? Supporting administrative measures against
"hard core" radicals? Providing new informants for the
FBI? Or contributing to the Committee's own intelli-
gence-gathering mission?

But, first, how real was the threat to freedom in February 1971, when the statement was circulated? Was the
Committee—in collusion with the CAC and university
officials— creating a panic through the pretense that the
"threats" were increasing alarmingly? After all, the numbers of students involved in demonstrations had dimin-
ished significantly in the 7 months since the troops were
withdrawn from Cambodia. Also, the Committee statement had been preceded by *seven or eight long years of
protests* directed against faculty who justified racial inequality or served the government war machine. Everyone knew the identities of the professors being targeted
by students or non-students— regardless of whether they
read the CAC bulletin.

Arthur Jensen, for instance, had been under attack
ever since his article, "How Much Can We Boost IQ and
Scholastic Achievement?" appeared almost two years
earlier in the 1969 issue of the *Harvard Educational Review*, claiming that the differences in I.Q. scores between whites and blacks are primarily due to the genetic
inferiority of the blacks.[15] It is worth noting that his article consumed almost all of the winter 1964 edition of the
Harvard Educational Review. Furthermore, if anyone at
Berkeley missed his article, they could read essays that
treated it seriously in *U.S. News and World Report*,

---

15 Jensen, Arthur, 1969. "How Much Can We Boost IQ and
   Scholastic Achievement?" *Harvard Educational Review* 69
   (Winter) pp. 1–123.

Time, Newsweek and *Life,* along with 14 million other readers who bought these publications—not to mention the millions who read it in their doctors' offices.

Also, in 1971, Richard Herrnstein, a Harvard psychology professor well known by criminologists for his notoriously racist theory of crime,[16] agreed with Jensen's article and wrote about its policy implications in *Atlantic Monthly.* He said that special government programs to assist in the health and education of African Americans were ill advised. Shortly thereafter, Eric Sevareid, the CBS prime-time news commentator, went on national television to say that it had been shown scientifically how some people were less educable than others, and that we should rethink federal policy and priorities.

In addition, Berkeley faculty and students who didn't read the national magazines or hear Eric Sevareid must have seen the front page of *The Daily Californian,* on May 11, 1969, after Jensen's article had been published. The front-page story, "Prominent Psychologists Oppose Jensen," printed a statement signed by notable psychologists, including the president of the American Psychological Association, attacking the scientific validity of Jensen's work.

Moreover, Scalapino and Teller had been denounced throughout the late Sixties. And, again, if anyone was still uninformed, *The Daily Californian,* only days before the Academic Freedom Committee's complaint was

---

16 *The Bell Curve: Intelligence and Class Structure in American Life* (New York: Free Press, 1994), coauthored with Charles Murray, is the most well known publication based on Herrnstein's theory. Many articles indicated this work is methodologically unsound. For a definitive refutation of *The Bell Curve,* see Stephen Jay Gould, *The Mismeasure of Man.* New York: W.W. Norton & Co. 1996.

circulated, had reported that members of a self-styled "War Crimes Commission" had leafleted Scalapino's class, accusing him of war crimes. Yet even though a Commission member demanded that Scalapino answer the charges when he entered the classroom, *The Daily Californian* reported that the members left the class and did not disrupt his lecture.[17]

The San Francisco Bay Guardian, on June 11, 1970 —during the Cambodian crisis and eight months prior to the 1971 memo about threats to academic freedom—had devoted a section to "The Bay Area War Machine," listing Scalapino as the head of "the most notorious project" devoted to third-world counter insurgency. The *Guardian* quoted a letter of resignation protesting "Pentagon involvement," written by Gerald O. Berreman, a UC Berkeley anthropologist who had also served on the project. Berreman wrote, "In the context of the illegal involvement of this country in the war in Vietnam, I cannot accept research money from an agency whose prima-

---

17 This incident seems blown out of proportion in the Academic Senate's deliberations. First, as indicated, the Mulford Act gave campus authorities and Berkeley police the right to eject non-students from the campus. Second, this incident is the *only one* actually cited in the Senate deliberations and none of the self-styled faculty "witnesses" who said they had seen this disruption were questioned. Furthermore, some professors, who failed to win a majority, tried to amend the resolution so that the incident would be considered an allegation rather than a fact. Finally, the description of this incident in "Berkeley Activist Ordered Off," *Daily Californian*, January 29, 1971, raises questions about its validity. This article indicates that activists had addressed the class *before* the session actually began and they mentioned they would be available *after* the session. If any "disruption" occurred *during* the class, a non-student may not have been the cause; consequently, "disruption" in this case may be comparable to the Cornell incident, which involve academic freedom for students and which had been discussed in a previous Chapter.

ry interest and purpose is the prosecution of that war and the furtherance of policies which are likely to lead to similar wars including wars in the very area of my research endeavor."

Again, within this short time frame, on March 5, 1971, the Committee on Academic Freedom issued another memo reminding Shelly Messinger, Acting Dean of the Criminology School, about its February communiqué. In this memo, the Committee requested administrators, department chairs and deans from every major academic unit, to provide "material" relevant to their inquiry into internal threats to academic freedom. It added that the scope of its investigation was *not being confined* to threatening incidents, and it wanted suggestions for developing "a broader perspective" to be "delivered personally or in writing." Since no instance mentioned by the Committee's original statement about internal threats to freedom indicated a faculty member being responsible for such threats, this deceitful expansion of its original mandate assumedly had a more sinister purpose, namely, mapping the distribution and identities of political dissenters and their departments throughout the campus.

Apropos of sinister purposes, two months before the Committee was created, UC Regent Max Rafferty, candidly admitted to the press that "unpublicized moves" were under way to remove college professors involved in "objectionable" campus activities.[18] Rafferty said, "If the cause remains – more student violence and dissent – there will be more dismissed." "They're are [sic] quietly going through that now on more and more campuses," he added. Regarding 14 professors who had recently been fired from Fresno State College, Rafferty sarcasti-

---

18 Rafferty had lost his Superintendent of Education position. He had just been defeated in a statewide election.

cally remarked, "More and more of the loose nuts on the faculties are going to be weeded out."[19] Meanwhile, the California legislature had targeted student movements by passing more legislation against students than any other state in the Union.

On this issue, *The New York Times* reported that "faculty cells" were emerging on university campuses to cope with student unrest. This development at UC Berkeley was accelerated by Governor Reagan's cuts in university funding. Facing the threat to personal security imposed by these cuts, some faculty, especially those who had remained silent—as many had done in the McCarthy era—supported the counter-reformists. They joined the growing academic lynch mob by denying tenure or renewals to the most visible anti-war faculty members, Richard Lichtman, Michael Leiserson and Kerrigan Prescott.[20]

Simultaneously, the leaders of the mob institutionalized repression by getting the Academic Senate to protect their interests. From a legal point of view, however, this protection was unnecessary. The Mulford Act, passed by the California State legislature to cope with student unrest, enabled the campus police to arrest a non-student who had challenged Scalapino in the classroom, escort him off-campus and charge him with a crime. Protection against harassment outside the campus was also covered by criminal law.

Given these legal safeguards, what in the world necessitated the Committee's alarming message and justifi-

---

19 "Dissident Profs: Rafferty Views Faculty Firings," *San Francisco Chronicle*, Dec 19, 1970.

20 Later, Stephen Talbot in the Native American Studies program was added to this list.

cation for disciplinary rules? The chain of events inescapably points to its desire to intimidate and search out political dissidents and to deflect attention from threats to these dissidents by "friendly fascists" on the faculty.

ACADEMIC FREEDOM & WAR CRIMES

To realize the enormity of the harm veiled by this stage-managing of academic freedom, and to put it in perspective, we must return to the final days of the free speech crisis. On December 8, 1964—five days after mass arrests in Sproul Hall had produced a campus-wide strike and one day after the spectacular failure of Kerr's convocation at the Greek Theatre—the Academic Senate resolved to end the "free speech crisis" by granting amnesty to the arrested students. Despite the Regents' opposition,[21] the Senate also voted to allow political speech and activity on campus.[22] The faculty overwhelmingly agreed that this was the only hope of settling "one of the most agonizing, shattering and potentially destructive experiences that any American university has ever had to pass through."[23]

When the Senate met in Wheeler auditorium, thousands of students massed in front of Wheeler Hall and packed its corridors. Loudspeakers immediately in-

---

21 The Regents, however, did not overturn the Senate's decisions.

22 These activities, as indicated previously, were subject to "time, place and manner" rules preventing students from disrupting "the normal functions" of the university.

23 Professor McClosky expressed this judgment. See the proceedings of the meeting, in UCB Academic Senate, 1964. (The proceedings were transcribed from an audiotape. The pages of the copy provided by the Bancroft Library archives are not numbered.)

formed the students of the faculty vote and, upon emerging from Wheeler Hall, the professors passed single-file through a cheering ecstatic crowd. "Many of us were crying as we applauded. Many of them were crying too," students reported. Although some professors complained the vote had been extorted by student pressure, university developments sweeping across the nation showed that that vote signified "the most consequential decision made by a university faculty in that era."[24]

Unlike the Cornell Senate two years later, the Berkeley professors had spent little time debating the question of amnesty. Instead, they argued whether the content of political speech and activity should be restricted. Although the majority had favored a "free speech" resolution offered by the Senate's Academic Freedom Committee, which did not restrict content, Lewis Feuer, from Philosophy and Sociology Departments, wanted the resolution modified. He proposed an amendment that only permitted activities "directed to no immediate act of force or violence."

Granting freedom of speech without this restriction, Feuer insisted, would allow a student Ku Klux Klan chapter to organize actions for defacing Jewish synagogues and Negro and Catholic churches. He prophesized that a free speech resolution without this restriction would encourage circumstances similar to those that helped destroy freedom and democracy in Germany during the thirties. Nazi students had claimed immunity from university authorities, which could do nothing, when they organized their attacks on Jews, liberals, Democrats and Socialists, according to Feuer.

---

24 See the commentary on an afterward to the proceedings cited above.

Carl Landauer, an economist who became a founding member of the CAC, supported Feuer's amendment.[25] He reminded the Senate of how hard it was to resist the Regents during the McCarthy period. He felt that granting free speech without Feuer's amendment would make resistance to the Regents totally indefensible.

Professor Arnon, a cell physiologist and another founding member of the CAC, backed Feuer's amendment. He declared the Senate was being blackmailed by a student mob determined to fight for their principles even if they destroyed themselves and the university. He mentioned rumors that outside groups would be coming to the campus at Berkeley if student demands were granted. He asked rhetorically what would the Senate do if students invited "outsiders"—such as a "President or Chairman of a prominent civil liberties organization"— to join their campus rallies?[26]

Despite these arguments, the majority believed the amendment would perpetuate the conflict between students and authorities. David Rytinn, from the Speech Department, observed that if students prepared boycotts or sit-ins or picketing against the outside community in the name of civil liberties, Feuer's amendment would render them again subject to the same kind of punitive threats and arrests as led to the crisis in the first place. The amendment was considered so vague that civil disobedience could be called "force and violence."

Bernard Diamond, identified as a psychiatrist in the

25 ~~Yet Landauer~~ agreed with the majority about the necessity for amnesty. "Mistakes have been made from all sides and the only conclusion we can draw is no further penalties," he said.

26 See UCB Academic Senate, 1964.

27 Later, Diamond's joint appointments included the School of

jections. First, he said the criminal law adequately covers acts of force and violence and neither the Senate nor the Regents have any business replacing the law. Second, the courts provide adequate means for administering and interpreting the law; and neither Senate committees nor administration should invade a territory that does not properly belong to them. Third, the definition of force and violence in relationship to civil disobedience is an exceedingly complex one; and the faculty or university "do not and will never have the necessary machinery for the implementation of and interpretation of the individual acts which may be relevant to this."

Furthermore, many felt the U.S. Constitution and Supreme Court decisions already provided acceptable criteria for judging free speech. Joseph Tussman, from the Department of Philosophy, dared to ask, suppose a person advocates violence but does it in a context in which there is not the slightest danger it will come about? Is there any reason why the authorities should stop that even if their concern is violence?

Upon objecting to Feuer's amendment, Owen Chamberlain, from the Department of Physics, made an important point. He said the students are proud of their use of civil disobedience because it puts high value on the lives of others and at the same time low value on the arbitrary rules of men. They feel the necessity of having their views heard yet believe there is little that would allow them the effectiveness they feel their conviction warrants. "It is all very well for a committee of the faculty to say that the recent disorders have hindered the consideration of student proposals, yet I for one do not believe it. The students feel that they have had no legitimate channel open."

Law.

The Berkeley Senate had rejected Feuer's amendment; nevertheless, seven years later it basically approved a "force and violence" rationale similar to the one rejected in 1964. It departed dramatically in 1972 from the 1964 Senate's wishes by adopting hazy interpretations of "force and violence" rather than those based on the Constitution and criminal law.

However, between 1964 and 1972, the anti-war movement in Berkeley had expanded enormously and so had movements elsewhere. While these movements had repeatedly damned official accounts of the war, the major news media usually defended the government and willingly printed its lies. Nonetheless, significant breaks in media coverage occurred as early as December 1966, when *New York Times* Editor Harrison E. Salisbury filed dispatches from Hanoi. The foreign press had reported that the U.S. had escalated the bombing and civilian areas had been targeted. The administration denied the escalation while Pentagon releases said military targets near Hanoi might have been hit but any damage to the city itself was due to antiaircraft ordnance falling back upon the city. Salisbury's first dispatch refuted these lies. He reported that the center of the city had been bombed and the U.S. had been bombing North Vietnamese population centers since 1965. He wrote, "The government is waging a war of steel and fire in Vietnam. It should not treat the American people as a second adversary, to be kept at bay with a smoke screen of distortion and soothing syrup."

From 1967 on, newspapers, pamphlets, magazines and books exposed atrocities routinely committed by American units in Vietnam, mostly against civilians. Eyewitness accounts of the criminal policies being relentlessly pursued by US military were provided at the proceedings of the War Crimes Tribunal, organized by Bertrand Russell and held in Stockholm and Copenhagen. Vietnam veterans also provided first hand accounts and, in 1970, 2,000 veterans startled the nation by camping on the Mall in Washington DC and returning medals won in battle by tossing them onto the steps of the Capitol. A year later, Representatives Ron Dellums and John Conyers paraded eyewitnesses at a Congressional hearing on US war crimes.

Consequently, Americans were repeatedly informed about the war crimes being committed in Indochina.[28] They were told about the enormous numbers of civilians killed and wounded by US and ARVN air and artillery strikes; the creation of free-fire zones which were ineffective against the NLF but devastating to civilians; the forced relocation of millions of Vietnamese villagers into dreadful refugee camps and slums; the use of herbicides to destroy crops and presumably deprive the NLF of food, which proved disastrous for the rural population; the customary beatings, torture and killing of NLF and North Vietnamese prisoners of war, primarily by ARVN troops but tolerated by US advisors; the terrorism and assassination promulgated by the notorious Phoenix Program; and the atrocities committed by US troops that were rarely punished. Furthermore, in 1971, government fabrications were blown sky high when newspapers published articles based on a classified historical study, ordered by McNamara in 1967, of US involvement in Vietnam.

Daniel Ellsberg and Anthony Russo, who worked at the Rand Corporation, had secretly copied the study and its supporting documents in 1969. After pleading unsuccessfully with anti-war legislators like J. William Full-

---

28 The term, 'Indochina,' includes Vietnam, Laos and Cambodia.

bright, George McGovern and Paul (Pete) McCloskey to release the study, they sent excerpts to a handful of leading newspapers. The government tried to stop these newspapers from publishing and its legal battle with *The New York Times* went all the way to the Supreme Court, which ruled in favor of *The Times* in June 1971.

Dubbed *The Pentagon Papers,* the excerpts of the Rand study demonstrated that American Presidents had deceived, ignored or manipulated a Congress composed of individuals who were either complicit in this deceit or too cowardly to meet their responsibilities under the Constitution. Presidents Truman, Eisenhower, Kennedy, Johnson and Nixon progressively committed US military resources to a criminal war of aggression against the Vietnamese. Truman provided military equipment on a large scale to the French colonial government, to be used against Vietnam rebels. To encourage the breakdown of the Geneva settlement between the French and Vietnamese, the Eisenhower administration undermined their negotiations. Kennedy encouraged the overthrow and assassination of President Ngo Dinh Diem of South Vietnam and his replacement by army officers.[29] He also initiated covert warfare, which was escalated into open warfare by Johnson whose plans for further action in 1964 produced the Tonkin Gulf incident.[30] For years afterward, Nixon followed up this incident by encouraging the calculated deceitful manipulation of public opinion. To disarm public opposition to the war and boost Nixon's reelection chances, for instance, Kissinger lied a few days before the 1972 election when he announced:

29 Members of his family and cabinet were also assassinated in this CIA backed operation.

30 But this incident did not initiate US aggression. Telford Taylor (*Nuremberg and Vietnam,* 174) states that 15,000 troops were already stationed in Vietnam when Johnson took office.

"Peace is at hand!" But the negotiations with the NLF and North Vietnamese collapsed shortly after the November election. Then, in the middle of the next month and through Christmas, Nixon ordered 18 days of carpet-bombing aimed at homes, hospitals and civilians in Hanoi and Haiphong.[31]

The Pentagon Papers proved conclusively that the government had waged a "war of aggression" in Vietnam—a war crime according to Nuremberg precedents. Before the Papers were published, General Telford Taylor, the chief prosecuting counsel at the Nuremberg trials, in *Nuremberg and Vietnam: An American Tragedy*, had difficulty deciding whether the United States had committed the crime of aggression, because the information to make an informed legal judgment about its possible guilt had not been disclosed. Although the Nuremberg tribunal was equipped with "virtual libraries of the defeated governments' most secret papers,"[32] the documents proving the United States' aggression in Vietnam had not been available until *The Pentagon Papers* were published in 1971.

About 36 people worked on the Rand study and most of them were military officers. All of them including Ellsberg had served in Vietnam.[33] The study contained a 3,000-page analysis, to which 4,000 pages of officially

31 During this time, a number of B2-Bomber pilots refused to fly missions.

32 Taylor (*Nuremberg and Vietnam*, 120.), said: "The Nuremberg and Tokyo judgments were rendered by international tribunals on a *post mortem* basis (all too literally), surrounded by virtual libraries of the defeated governments' most secret papers."

33 See, "Conversation with Daniel Ellsberg." In Harry Kreisler, "Presidential Decisions and Public Dissent: Reflections of the Vietnam War." *Conversations with History*. Institute of International Studies, UC Berkeley, July 29, 1988.

classified documents were appended. One did not have to be a professor at an elite university to realize that these documents, beyond a doubt, proved the anti-war movements and their unofficial war crime tribunals had been right all along. The documents demonstrated that isolated soldiers were not responsible for the use of air-borne weapons of mass destruction or search-and-destroy missions that killed every living thing in sight. Nor were these crimes merely committed by officers— like Lieutenants William Calley and Bob Kerrey[34]—who were following orders or caught up in the frenzy of war. The crimes were inevitable consequences of policies planned and executed by officials at the highest levels of government.

The Papers confirmed that the United States had lied when it justified its invasion of Vietnam on behalf of a sovereign power. The South Vietnamese government was not a sovereign power. Originally, the "zones" distinguishing Northern and Southern Vietnam were based on a cease-fire agreement pending a democratic election. According to Taylor,

> The Geneva agreement of 1954 did not purport to establish two nations, but two 'zones,' and explicitly declared that 'the military demarcation line is provisional and should not in any way be interpreted as constituting a political or territorial boundary. It was the basis for a cease-fire, and the purpose of the zones was specified as 'regrouping.' The agreement further

---

34 In 2001, the American public was informed about another atrocity—this time involving the ex-Senator Bob Kerrey who commanded a unit that killed every civilian in a Vietnamese village even though it was not confronted by armed opposition.

> provided for 'free' nationwide elections, to
> be held in 1956, as the basis for a
> government based on 'the principles of
> independence, unity and territorial
> integrity.'[35]

But, the *Papers* showed the United States encouraged the corrupt South Vietnamese government break that agreement because it knew the government could not obtain domestic support for that tactic democratically. Then, after deciding that the government also incapable of winning the ensuing civil war, the U.S. selected Vietnamese officers who had served in the French colonial forces, and engineered the military *coup d'état*.[36] Consequently, the US war crimes were not restricted to the manner in which it fought the Vietnamese War. They originated in a "crime of aggression" because the US had invaded Vietnam to maintain colonial surrogates during a civil war.

The growing number of people raising questions about criminality at the highest level of government included Taylor, the Nuremberg prosecutor. Even though he restricted his judgment to My Lai, free strike zones, treatment of prisoners and other atrocities committed by ground troops, he pointed out that if standards applied in the prosecution of German and Japanese war crimes were applied impartially to American statesmen and bureaucrats managing the Vietnam War, they would most

---

35 Nuremberg and Vietnam: An American Tragedy, p.102.

36 See Young, *Vietnam Wars*, 1945–1990, 159. In early 1966, a U.S. intelligence assessment noted later, there was an "almost total absence of any organized popular support, or even sympathy for the American-backed regime," quoted in Kahin, *Intervention*, 421.

likely be found guilty.[37] While clarifying the grounds for this judgment, he dismissed the argument that these Americans were innocent because they were ignorant of the atrocities committed by U.S. forces. He said that after March 16, 1968, when soldiers in the field reported a number of atrocities, (including the My Lai massacre) to their superior officers, nobody could reasonably claim to have been uniformed.

Christopher Hitchens, in the most recent and compelling indictment of Kissinger, goes further than Taylor. His book, *The Trial of Henry Kissinger*, reviewed the overwhelming amount of evidence for the crimes committed in Indochina.[38] To back his indictment, he employs eyewitnesses, documents released under the Freedom of Information Act, previously unpublished correspondence, transcriptions of the "Nixon tapes" and testimony given to Congressional committees. Kissinger's criminal acts, according to Hitchens, began in 1964 when he prolonged the war by secretly ensuring the failure of peace negotiations between President Johnson's administration and Vietnamese representatives. While the CAC and Academic Freedom Committee were conducting their campaign against the Berkeley anti-war activists in 1972, Kissinger was designing and managing policies killing and wounding at least three million civilians in Indochina alone.[39]

---

37 Telford Taylor, *Nuremberg and Vietnam,* 154–182.

38 Christopher Hitchens, *The Trial of Henry Kissinger.*

39 The first few names on the Vietnam War Memorial in Washington, DC, are dated 1954 when the U.S. began to support French forces. Since the last few are dated 1975, the U.S. was involved in the Vietnam conflict for 21 years. Furthermore, when civilians are included, the true Vietnamese casualties may have reached 4,000,000.

What about the university administrators and faculty who condemned both the Berkeley war crimes tribunal and the expression of anti-war sentiments in classrooms? Weren't these people morally culpable. They certainly could not claim ignorance of the atrocities being committed in Indochina. The publication of excerpts from the *Pentagon Papers*— in leading newspapers and in 1.5 million copies of a paperback edition published by the *NY Times*—had informed the university community about the government's deceitful manipulation of public opinion. These and other publications indicated that the CAC and Academic Freedom Committee were not impartial apolitical agencies, justifiably defending the university as "a house of reason." They were an extension, in civil society, of government policies aimed at obstructing justice and enabling serial killers to commit crimes with impunity.

In 1964, the Senate majority rejected Feuer's amendment and his absurd comparisons between students in Berkeley and Nazi students who had invoked free speech principles to claim immunity for their attacks on Jews, liberals, Democrats, Communists and Socialists. Actually, the Nazi government had granted their immunity and enforced it with assaults, torture, prisons and concentration camps. American federal, state and university authorities, on the other hand, steadfastly opposed the anti-war movement in Berkeley. Along with their allies on the university faculty, they discouraged free speech and employed a double standard when defending particular faculty members from criticism. These members were tacitly accorded institutional "immunity" despite accusations of complicity in the greatest crimes recognized by modern nations.

6 | Moving In for the Kill

The early nineteen seventies witnessed numerous in-stances of campus repression. In one instance, the San Jose State economics department, with a diversified and balanced faculty (including free marketers, Keynesians, institutionalists and Marxists) was taken over by the administration. Threatened by the free play of ideas, the administration refused to allow the faculty to pick the chairperson, fired four junior faculty members and denied tenure to another faculty member.

Even visiting professors at other universities were affected. At UC Santa Barbara, for instance, the administration, without good cause, in the Fall of 1970 terminated Maurice Zeitlin as a Visiting Sociologist because he had engaged in anti-war protests at the University of Wisconsin.[1] Protesting this case, the department chair, Walter Buckley, noted other instances on his campus.

---

1 Zeitlin was terminated even though his visiting appointment had been approved "without salary" and even though the University of Wisconsin had never charged him with an infraction of university regulations after he had participated in a faculty strike over the Cambodian invasion. See, "Zeitlin Case: statement from Soc. Dept." Editorial page, *UCSB Daily Nexus*, Thursday, October 8, 1970.

One outstanding case, never public, included the Chancellor's repeated refusal to grant the request of twice Nobel Prize winner Linus Pauling—made through the Chemistry Department—for a small piece of laboratory space in which to carry on his research.[2] Another outstanding action, Dr. John Seeley, former chairman at Brandeis and internationally known scholar, was refused a courtesy use of the facilities for research. Both of these men are considered "politically controversial."

On the Berkeley campus, the opportunity for legitimating the purge of the Criminology School presented itself just after Messinger submitted a proposal to the Graduate Council, requesting formal ratification for a curriculum leading to a Doctor of Philosophy. The doctorate provided by the School was a professional doctorate; hence, Doctor of Criminology rather than Doctor of Philosophy. Messinger's proposal was intended for students who had acquired greater theoretical sophistication and research training in order to "focus on problems of generating knowledge about crime and criminal justice."[3]

Before we recount how the counter-reformists seized this moment, the background to this proposal should be detailed. To begin with, the planning for a Ph.D. program had been a logical culmination of changes in faculty and curriculum. The School opened in 1949 and, until 1960, August Vollmer and O.W. Wilson essentially de-

---

2 Subsequently, Prof. Pauling received an appointment at UC San Diego.

3 Messinger circulated this proposal among the Criminology faculty and asked them to keep it confidential until their comments were incorporated and it was sufficiently polished to send on to the Graduate Council. See Sheldon Messinger, "Program for a Graduate Studies in Criminology for a Ph.D., December 1970."

veloped the School as a career academy for professional managers of the criminal justice system, much as West Point trains elite army officers. The School was imbued with an uncritical Cold War ideology[4] and, in addition, the entire faculty had been recruited from the criminal justice system and understood the School as a service institution for that system. However, threatened with the School's elimination for its narrow vocational aims, it was reorganized in 1961 by Dean Lohman.

Under Lohman, an interdisciplinary faculty concerned with the social, psychological and legal aspects of crime partially replaced the earlier managerial emphasis. Changing the priorities to favor the graduate program rather than the undergraduate, the School trained research personnel, college and university teachers and professional policy makers.

In the ensuing period, most faculty were social scientists and legal scholars; and, some, stirred by the changing political climate, began to raise fundamental questions about crime and criminal justice itself. By 1968, Lohman himself believed, "Many of the problems confronting us today have a significance quite different from the meanings traditionally ascribed to them and to the social contexts to which they relate." He said it would be "profitable to examine the agencies, institu-

---

4 When the American Military Government Documents were declassified, Falco Werkentin, a German criminologist, sent us two memos written by Vollmer who, after Germany's surrender, had been assigned the task of monitoring the West Berlin police department. In one memo, Vollmer decided to leave the decision about whether to hire police applicants who were members of the Nazi party up to local German authorities. In the other document, he decided the American military government would not allow anyone suspected of communist sympathies to be hired by the police department.

tions, and organizations to which we uncritically sub-
scribe and to apply the ideas of alienation and estrange-
ment to the institutional framework itself." In fact, he
declared, "The changing patterns of crime are a reflec-
tion of far-reaching changes in American community life
. . . It is not likely that we will be successful in controlling crime without seriously changing the organization
and administration of criminal justice."[5] Accordingly,
Lohman favored faculty members who could teach social science and professionally oriented courses that
transcended the narrow managerialism of the earlier era.

However, toward the end of 1968 Lohman died suddenly and Leslie Wilkins, the Associate Dean, became
Dean. Wilkins was greatly admired by students and faculty alike because of his high moral standards and professional dedication. He felt that the school was moving
in the right direction and encouraged faculty deliberations strengthening the broadened curriculum. He observed,

> The School has developed and is still in the
> course of developing a philosophy of
> operation which distinguishes the training of
> persons to enter a profession from that of
> training qualified persons to question basic
> assumptions which underlay professional
> activities through the use of research
> analysis.[6]

He supported the general belief that a Doctor of Philosophy in Criminology, centered on social science and re-

5 Joseph D. Lohman, "Crises of a Society in Ferment," *Crime and
   Delinquency*, January 1968, pp. 31-41.

6 The memo was addressed to the School's "Policy and Planning
   Committee," and it is dated, May 14, 1968.

search training, should be provided by the School.

Wilkins also set up a number of faculty committees to reorganize the curriculum. The reorganization went through various phases. By 1971, when the Sindler Committee attacked the School, the curriculum had broadened significantly.

But Wilkins's ethical principles placed him in an untenable position. As the "third world liberation" and "black power" protests escalated, the UCB authorities demanded his cooperation in policing and informing on the faculty.[7] Being asked to inform on the faculty who were cooperating with the strikers at that time placed Wilkins between "a rock and a hard place." On one occasion during the TWLF strike, when Schwendinger happened to be present, Wilkins received a call from an administrator who demanded the names of faculty refusing to teach in assigned classrooms.[8] Wilkin's shouted in reply to the caller: "I am not a policeman!" and slammed the phone down.[9]

Wilkins resigned in the aftermath of the third world strike. At a faculty meeting of the School of Criminology on February 24, 1969, he announced his decision:

---

7 Although the administration eventually relented and instituted ethnic studies, black studies and affirmative action programs, it resisted these reforms. To overcome this resistance, a strike was called. Eventually, thousands of students boycotted classes and sympathetic faculty refused to teach even though they were repelled by arson and vandalism reportedly committed by a small group of black students.

8 These faculty members did not hold classes in their assigned rooms but some like Schwendinger held them in a religious center on the edge of the campus.

9 Schwendinger, who was in Wilkin's office at the time, witnessed his angry response.

> I have just informed Chancellor Heyns that I
> wish to be relieved of making the kind of
> decisions that seem to be required of deans
> during this crisis, and that I am resigning
> from the University at the end of the spring
> quarter. I trust the faculty and see my role as
> supporting them rather than spying on them,
> as seems required now. My decision to
> resign was based…on a cumulative series of
> political and personal pressures, the former
> having recently been brought to bear on the
> University and on the School. I feel the
> position of Dean in this School is a political
> one and I am not able to cope with such a
> setting.[10]

Wilkins finally left the School.[11] Sheldon Messinger then became Acting Dean and, taking up the task initiated by Wilkins, drafted the Ph.D. curriculum proposal with agreement from the faculty. This draft, however, was preceded by an unusual set of events. In 1971, the Dean of Graduate Studies, following traditional procedures for evaluating departments and professional schools, appointed the "Wolfgang Committee" composed of nationally renowned criminologists, Martin Wolfgang, Donald Riddle, Richard Myren and James Short, to evaluate the School. This committee, far from recommending the demise of the School, found it "healthier than ever before." It reported that the faculty was overworked and recommended limiting the size of the undergraduate program. But it undeniably found the School academically sound, the faculty stable, and even though some relations with outside agencies could be improved, student

---

10 Quoted in Wasserman, op cit., p. 50.

11 He accepted a job at the SUNY, Albany, School of Criminal Justice.

field placements in criminal justice agencies were generally fine. Wilkins was considered an excellent Dean, the students were firmly behind the School and the faculty and student moral was high. The committee, perhaps aware of Bowker's reservations about the School, suggested that he become more familiar with the faculty's sense of commitment and vision.[12]

After the School received the very favorable review by the Wolfgang Committee, the Ph.D. proposal was confidently forwarded for approval in 1971 to the Academic Senate and administration.

However, after discovering that notable criminologists had implicitly criticized him but not the School, Bowker left nothing to chance. With Elberg, the Dean of Graduate Studies, he formed his own committee composed, this time, of politically accommodating faculty members. Sindler, still raging over Cornell's reconciliation with African-American students, was appointed the Committee Chairman. Like Kenneth Starr's investigation of President Clinton, which began with Clinton's Arkansas associates, Sindler broadened the mission of the committee and joyfully served the Chancellor by devising every conceivable reason to destroy the School.

Since the evaluation by the Wolfgang Committee had praised the curricula and research developed by the School faculty, Sindler could not readily employ their professional standards to condemn the School on those grounds. Accordingly, Bowker ignored the events justifying the original rejection of the School's "vocational-

12 Report of the Visiting Committee on the School of Criminology to the Chancellor, University of California, Berkeley, California. December 17, 1971. Although the committee may have been selected while Heyns was still Chancellor, Bowker replaced him at beginning of the 1971 fall semester.

ism" prior to the 1960s and the subsequent appointment of Joseph D. Lohman. Since a vocational and technical-service school at Berkeley was a patently outdated relic, Lohman, you remember, had been given the task of reorganizing the curriculum. Nonetheless, Sindler embraced the School's archaic Charter as a police academy and forensic laboratory and used this prehistoric document to define the "professional mission" of the School. He claimed the School should be closed because it had abandoned its original mission and become too "academic"[13] even though this rationale, if applied generally, would have justified closing virtually every one of the professional schools at Berkeley.

To deal with the inevitable reaction to the report, Sindler armed his allies at the university by denouncing the courses taught by radicals, the organization of the School's curriculum and the quality of its teaching staff. He also criticized the large number of students attracted to its courses, the size of the graduate program, the objections raised by law-enforcement, and on and on. He said the undergraduate curriculum was disorganized even though it had been painstakingly reorganized and its core curriculum contained twice as many required courses as Sindler's Political Science Department in Berkeley.

The report could not stand scrutiny and subsequent review committees, individual faculty, the AFT faculty chapter, student organizations and student newspapers challenged every one of its critical observations. But the debate among the UCB faculty fixated on Sindler's seemingly apolitical criticisms of the School rather than

---

13 The Sindler committee shamelessly alleged that the PhD program request proved that the criminology faculty were abandoning their "professional" mission.

the politics producing his report. Since university functionaries and their political overlords backed Sindler, the report now provided counter-reformists with the ability to shift the terms of debate at will. Simultaneously, other faculty, including criminologists, could not, without personal risk, publicly challenge the tactics being made to legitimize the School by Bowker and his review committee.

7 | Platt Denied Tenure

S ome radicals at the School were socialists. Yet even though they were fond of revolutionary rhetoric, their activism was always based on nonviolent and reformist agendas. They informed the public and students about social class and racial inequities in criminal justice systems. They exposed sexist legal practices and promoted resources for women who were battered and raped. They fought to make police accountable through community control and civilian review boards. They participated in the struggle for prisoners' rights and opposed experimentation in prisons. They collaborated with anti-war movements and attacked university complicity in the military-industrial complex.

In a sensitive and thoughtful article about the Berkeley period, Platt asserts that the radicals tended toward ultraleftism, romanticism and a messianic utopianism.[1] But the word "tended," in this context, should be qualified because it glosses over significant political differ-

---

1 See, among others, Platt, Anthony M. 1991. "If We know, Then We Must Fight.' The Origins of Radical Criminology in the United States." Pp. 218–232 in *Radical Sociologists and the Movement: Experiences, Lessons, and Legacies*, edited by Marin Oppenheimer, Martin Murray, and Rhonda E. Levine. Philadelphia: Temple University Press. See pp. 227–228.

ences among the radicals—including the socialists. It also pays no attention to the seemingly paradoxical combination of revolutionary rhetoric and reformist agendas that characterized student movements in the Sixties. Despite their fondness for this kind of rhetoric, the radicals at the School were for all practical purposes "radical democrats" or "social democrats"—not Pop-Leninists.

Platt, of course, has never contended that ultraleftists, romanticists or messianic utopians killed the School of Criminology even though "respectable witnesses" at the scene of the crime point to the usual suspects. But the scene of the murder is like *film noir*, darkly lit and filled with characters who stubbornly refuse to see the frame-up that obstructed justice by shunting the investigation into a search for red herrings.

The university administration's denial of tenure for Platt provides additional evidence about who actually committed the crime. Since this denial was a gross violation of academic freedom, the university publications, mass media and everyone attending the School followed Tony Platt's tenure case. His undergraduate years were spent at Oxford University in England. He received the 1967 Richard McGee Award as "Outstanding Graduate Student" and was considered among the most brilliant students to graduate from the School. He joined the faculty toward the end of the Sixties after being employed at the University of Chicago and his academic record justified an accelerated promotion. In the early Seventies, the senior faculty, two Deans, and the Committee on Privilege and Tenure had recommended his tenure. Nonetheless, Platt's name was deleted from the recommendations list sent to the Regents after he was arrested and beaten by police and falsely accused of criminal acts.

The lies justifying the demise of the School and the identification of the usual suspects were particularly evident in Platt's case. What, if anything, were his crimes? Platt and a friend, Tom Hayden, had joined a demonstration marking the anniversary of the savage police reaction against the "People's Park" demonstration. Platt's sworn account, written immediately after his encounter with police, also illustrates how customary police brutality had become at Berkeley:

> I was first arrested at 4:00PM on Saturday, May 15,1971. Three cops were chasing a young man over Bancroft Avenue and onto the campus, just north of Sproul Hall. I ran over to watch as they beat and handcuffed the man ... Schneider, a plainclothes campus cop was one of the three involved in beating the handcuffed prisoner.[2] While this was happening, other cops were saturating the area with tear gas, which seemed to have little effect on dispersing people. [Schneider] said, 'I've got two more maggots in the car. I'll bring them down' (into the police station). [He] pushed by me and knocked my glasses to the floor, breaking the frames. He went over to a police car parked on the east side of Barrows Lane, next to Sproul Hall. He told Tom Hayden and Jeff Gerth [who were arrested in the midst of the chaos][3] to 'get out, you maggots.'

---

2 Platt's statement identified the plainclothesman's name but he was not sure of the spelling.

3 The FBI had distributed photographs of SDS and other notable personalities. Police were ready to arrest these leaders on trumped-up charges when they were spotted during demonstrations.

He pushed the two prisoners around and cursed and pushed Platt as he brought them towards the police station. Platt asked him what he was doing and he replied, "Get out of here. Fuck off maggot!"

Platt went to the campus police department to register a complaint about police brutality. However, when he said that he wanted to see Chief Beal or "somebody else" to file a complaint, the policeman on guard at the entrance grabbed him, twisted his arm, and led him to a holding area. Platt explained, "There were four other persons in the holding area [including Hayden, who had been beaten, and Gerth] all standing facing the wall." He was also told to face the wall, with his hands against the wall and legs spread apart. "Somebody pushed my hands and legs wider so that my body was taut and stretched," he reported. Then, Schneider, catching him completely by surprise, punched him in the lower right abdomen. Platt protested, "The blow hurt because it was well placed and I was completely vulnerable. I dropped to the floor and two cops immediately picked me up and ordered me to stand against the wall again." Following the attack, he not only felt nauseous but his stomach hurt for hours. He was then charged with "interfering with an officer."

Platt was fingerprinted, booked and released on bail. He walked to the street where he had parked his car prior to the demonstration. But someone had slashed his tires and smashed his rear-view mirror. (No other car on that street had been vandalized.) While Platt was inspecting the adjacent cars, a patrol car suddenly pulled up with two policemen. One pointed at a car next to Platt's and identified it as his own. He accused Platt of intending to vandalize his [the policeman's] car. Although the policeman was repeatedly told that the vandalized car *was Platt's* own *car*, he handcuffed Platt, beat him, took him to the station and beat him again. He was fingerprinted and, incredible as it may seem, booked this time for committing "malicious mischief to an automobile."

Platt had been booked on false charges and criminally assaulted by the police. Nevertheless, the university administration invoked disciplinary rules against him to justify removing his name from the tenure list sent to the Regents. Subsequently, however, at his trial in the Berkeley municipal court, the judge dismissed the charges and a police department document substantiating Platt's mistreatment was publicized.[4]

After the criminal charges against Platt were dismissed, the administration invented new reasons for denying his tenure. UC President Heyns had called Platt "immature." His replacement, UCB Chancellor Bowker, cited Platt's political disagreements with local police agencies as one reasons for denying tenure. He also said that he had conducted his own review of Platt's merits, in part, based on a secret file not made available to review committees.

In a 1972 memo, Bowker provides further examples of his cynical disregard of the rules of fair play.[5] He emphasized negative student evaluations and suggested that students were only "stimulated and engaged" by his classes because they shared Platt's political bias. Unbelievably, even though Platt was considered one of the finest students to have graduated from the Criminology

---

4   During the following months, Takagi and Schwendinger circulated a letter describing the Platt case that asked for donations to offset his legal costs.

5   Memo to Budget Committee, from Chancellor Albert H. Bowker, May 1, 1972.

School, Bowker reached back to Platt's student days and, after examining his transcripts, claimed that Platt should have taken more graduate courses in criminology and other subjects. He even scrutinized Platt's qualifying examination for the Doctorate degree and lamely found a scribbled notation by a respected faculty member[6] who praised Platt's answer but observed that he really didn't answer the question.[7]

Bowker cited Platt didn't deserve tenure because of his political disagreements with local police agencies. He also objected to Platt's speeches at rallies and his testimony as a citizen and "expert" before the Berkeley City Council. Platt had participated with others in a successful attempt to prevent purchase of a police helicopter by the City of Berkeley. The helicopter could have been used for controlling demonstrations but would have had little value—especially in light of its great cost—in fighting street crime. Yet Bowker called Platt a "demagogue" for saying the helicopter would especially target Third World members and campus communities and thereby "accelerate the trend toward police militarism and a garrison state." (Such comments, it will be recalled, were made when the memory was still fresh of a National Guard helicopter spraying tear gas on demonstrators at the Student Union Building and Sproul Plaza.)

Platt had campaigned, albeit unsuccessfully, for (1) a reorganization of the Berkeley police to ensure community control and for (2) a citizen's police-review board

---

6 This faculty member was an "outside member," from another department, required for conducting qualifying and oral doctoral exams.

7 The faculty member, however, did approve of Platt's overall performance and signed his name to the formal documents noting that Platt had passed the examination.

that would handle complaints about police. His right to engage in these activities was supported by constitutional law. Yet, Bowker now claimed Platt was unprofessional because he undermined police morale.

AFT Local 1474 denounced Bowker's barefaced violations of academic freedom. It devoted an entire edition of its newspaper, *University Guardian,* to the Platt case. "BOWKER BLOCKS PROMOTION—TRAMPLES ACADEMIC FREEDOM" headlined the first page. Bowker's outrageous comments about Platt's writings, teaching and political activities were itemized on page two. The third page detailed the Senate's Privilege and Tenure Committee's majority finding that Bowker had violated Platt's academic freedom. Pages four and five scathingly reviewed the hypocrisy and spelled out the lies behind Bowker's refusal to recommend tenure. Page four was particularly informative: It printed an unsolicited statement, given to a Senate Committee by a visiting scholar who, as early as May 22, 1972, attended a dinner hosted by Bowker. The scholar said that the after-dinner conversation centered on Platt's case for over half an hour. He added,

> Chancellor Bowker said that the School of Criminology did not belong on the Berkeley campus and that he would like to get rid of it. He said budget cuts necessitated eliminating certain departments and that weak or second-rate departments would be the first to go. In discussing his grounds for considering the School of Criminology to be of little value, Bowker said that 'all the important law enforcement officials in the area with one exception, the Sheriff of San

Francisco, said they had no use for it.'[8]

Since, Bowker formed the Sindler Committee in November, his candid remarks six months earlier at the dinner indicate that the Committee was a fraud. Its members were chosen because they would give Bowker what he wanted.

The final page of the *University Guardian* featured a letter from Leon Wofsy, Professor of Immunology and President of the Local, which drew parallels between Nixon's Constitutional violations and Bowker's confidential letter to the Senate Budget Committee earlier in 1972. Wofsy declared,

> No one considering the sequence of events and, above all, reading that letter, can escape the sense of being exposed to another episode of life as seen from inside executive chambers in Richard Nixon's Washington. In fact, there can be hardly a doubt about how 95% of the Berkeley campus would react if this were indeed a tale out of Washington: a story of gross abuse of executive power and privilege, of confidential files on enemies, of invitation to improper political intervention by law enforcement agencies, of legal maneuvers and interminable delays, of employment of budget and administrative manipulation to violate rights and punish an individual.[9]

Wofsy unsuccessfully urged the Academic Senate to

8 "Unacceptable to Police Agencies." *University Guardian*, AFT Local 1474, November 1973, p. 4.

9 Leon Wofsy, "Open Letter to UC Faculty." *University Guardian*, AFT Local 1474. *Nov. 1973*, p. 8.

strongly censure Bowker and call on the Chancellor to "restore without delay" Platt's nomination to tenure rank.

To obtain tenure, Platt fought an exhausting, unsuccessful, four-year battle with the Chancellor's office. The Academic Senate's Privilege and Tenure Committee again and again reviewed his qualifications decided in his favor. It concluded that the Chancellor had violated Platt's academic freedom because "political criteria" were a factor in his case. But the administration rejected the Committee's findings.[10] *Platt was never given tenure at UCB.*

---

10 "Will Faculty Defend Academic Freedom?" *University Guardian*, American Federation of Teachers, October 1974.

8 | The Legitimacy Crisis

P redictably, Sindler had admirers. In the Foreword to *The Closing of the American Mind: How Higher Education Has Failed Democracy and Impoverished the Souls of Today's Students,* Allen Bloom wrote: "I want to express my admiration for Allan P. Sindler, who has been for me the model of the selfless university man. His lifelong behavior proves that the enterprise is still possible and worthwhile."[1] That "worthwhile" enterprise, unsurprisingly, still aimed at revitalizing the climate of the Fifties when, according to Bloom, women were distinguished from men because they were feminine and elite universities only served students who had the "personal advantages" in money and talent that merited a liberal education. For Bloom, bringing back the past would compensate for the catastrophic Sixties—when spineless faculty refused to join the "brave band" who fought the rabble that dumped liberal education and allowed inner-city "barbarians" and affirmative action into the "house of reason."

---

1 Bloom states, "The Earhart Foundation and the John M. Olin Foundation have supported me as teacher and scholar for a long time, and I am very grateful to their officers." These foundations are among the growing number of right-wing foundations supporting conservative academics.

Bloom taught at Cornell with Sindler in 1969 when African American students seized Willard Straight Hall.[2] In Bloom's view, Cornell's President, James A. Perkins, shared the blame for this "outrage" because he had supported affirmative action in 1967. Bloom said this support increased enrollment of black students (especially inner-city blacks) who were ill prepared "for the great intellectual and social challenges awaiting them in the university."

Bloom insisted that the Cornell faculty should have failed these students instead of passing them and thereby making them "recognizably second class citizens." He was further enraged by that "capitulation" because this stigma was neutralized by the Black Power movement. He claimed that the movement "hit the universities like a tidal wave" and it wrongly asserted that universities did not teach the truth. It claimed black students were second-class not because they were academically poor but because they were being forced to imitate white culture. "The way was opened for black students to live and study the black experience, to be comfortable, rather than be constrained by the learning accessible to man as man," Bloom moaned.

Bloom further alleged that black students extorted a reconciliation at gunpoint following the seizure of Willard Straight Hall. He noted approvingly that law professors, supported by the mass media, petitioned the Trustees to dismiss President Perkins because he had refused to summon police when the sit-in occurred. Perkins was forced to resign. (In later years, Tom Jones,

---

2 Bloom left Cornell for the University of Chicago where he wrote the book. It was riddled with inaccurate claims and pandered to popular prejudices; but it was lauded by the mass media and became a bestseller.

the black student leader whose threats panicked the group led by Sindler became a TIAA-CREF vice president. Afterwards, Jones obtained an annual salary of $2,000,000 at Smith Barney's and he graciously funded a Cornell scholarship in Perkins' name.)

Granted, Sindler, a political scientist, may not have fully agreed with Bloom but they undoubtedly shared similar views of affirmative action and women's, ethnic and black-studies programs. Bloom's opinions about these matters, of course, were easy to pin down because he wore them on his sleeve; however, since Sindler cultivated a cool air of impartiality, his opinions were not uncovered easily.

Still, Charles M. Lamb, another political scientist, was not taken-in by Sindler's public persona. With regard to Sindler's study of the Bakke "reverse discrimination" case,[3] he observed,

> Underneath what appears to be an objective study are signs of a pro-Bakke bias. First, of all the opinions written in the Bakke case, only Justice Brennan's anti-Bakke stance comes under direct fire. For example, Sindler characterizes the Brennan position as tautological, incomplete, misleading, fallacious, as an 'attempt to settle the matter by judicial fiat,' and as seeking to 'reconcile racial preferences and not reverse discrimination by defining reverse discrimination out of existence.'[4]

---

3   In this 'reverse discrimination' case, the Supreme Court concluded in a narrow 5-4 decision the minority quota program of the UC Davis Medical School was illegal.

4   Charles M. Lamb's 1979 review of Alan P. Sindler's Bakke, DeFunis, and Minority Admissions: The Quest for Equal

Although it is virtually impossible to prove "intent" (as opposed to readily observable data) in affirmative-action cases, Sindler insisted a person's intentions must be used to demonstrate proof of institutionalized racism and discrimination at the workplace.

Although Bloom's denunciation of the Sixties appeared a decade and a half after Sindler's academic-freedom memo and report, together they signified phases of the same conservative *putsch*. While attempting to contain the damage created by "barbarians" who "failed democracy" and "destroyed the souls of students," they demonized the Sixties. The damage, in their minds, was caused, above all, by radical intellectuals who at that time debunked patriotic myths, undermined customary beliefs supporting female inequality, portrayed universities as instruments of class and racial oppression, and exposed hypocrisies underlying corporate liberalism (the dominant ideology of advanced capitalist societies).

The Definition of Crime & the Crisis

Of course, radicals at the School contributed to this demystification of ruling institutions and ideology. Given their professional interests and outlooks, they naturally debunked the traditional rationales for class, gender and racially biased law enforcement policies. As political dissent intensified, their targets expanded. They began to include class control of government and America's political economy.

They even criticized legal definitions of crime. Schwendinger, for instance, was familiar with a long standing debate about the relation between criminology,

Opportunity. In *The American Political Science Review* 73 (December) 1161–1162.

the law, and the state. He felt that this debate had opened a Pandora's box and let loose fundamental questions about the nature and aims of criminology.

He said that criminology was the only discipline whose object of inquiry was imposed by the state. While church and state in the Middle Ages had defined the parameters of physics and astronomy, scientists in these fields today reject the role played previously by these authorities. Nevertheless, criminologists overwhelmingly take for granted that crime is defined by the law and sanctioned by the state.

He also was familiar with the work of an eminent criminologist, Edwin Sutherland, who believed that other definitions of crime were possible. Sutherland noted that "white collar crimes were committed by people who had the power to limit how their harmful acts could be prosecuted or whether these acts were even defined as a crime."[5] To justify his standpoint, Sutherland stressed that crime is generally regarded to be *socially harmful* conduct. The phrase "socially harmful" in this context implies that criminal acts such as murder or theft are, in principle, offenses offending *society at large* as well as an individual.

Schwendinger went further. If "crime" was considered socially harmful conduct, what about policies that lawmakers did not consider crimes even though they were caused by the suppression of human rights? And what about the popular usage of the word crime for great social harms that are not crimes by law simply because

---

5   For centuries, writers have noted the degree to which criminal codes target the poor and powerless rather than the rich and powerful. As Anatole France exclaimed, "The law in its majestic equality, forbids the rich and the poor to steal bread and to sleep under bridges."

powerful groups or classes determine what will be defined as crime? Also, if these great harms are produced by systemic characteristics of a social system, should that system be considered criminal?

Operational interpretations of definitions of crime were also problematic. Students at the School of Criminology took courses at the Law School. And to meet course requirements, they were submitting essays that condemned Nixon and Kissinger as war criminals. Their instructors rejected their essays and insisted that they were using the word crime unprofessionally. Nixon and Kissinger, in their view, were not war criminals until they had actually been found guilty in a court of law.

This kind of view had been expressed in the long-lost debate by a legal scholar, Paul Tappan, who contended that Edwin Sutherland, a criminologist, had no right to use the term white-collar crime to classify corporations not been found guilty of violating the law or not committed acts codified by criminal laws. Consequently, the Berkeley professors who shared Tappan's opinion were tightening the customary bonds that tied criminology to the state and its definitions of crime.

Schwendinger felt that Sutherland's objections were valid. But he felt that the notion of "social harm" had to be spelled out. He suggested that grounding definitions of crime in historically evolving conceptions of fundamental human rights might prove useful in making this break.

For example, when the Cambodian invasion occurred, Schwendinger had already drafted the article on the definition of crime but the invasion underscored its relevance. Students across the nation flew into a rage against the war. One-third of the colleges in the United States were shut down by demonstrations and walkouts. Ohio National Guardsmen killed four student protesters at Kent State, and two Mississippi students were killed at Jackson State. Nevertheless, even though Congress subsequently repealed the Gulf of Tonkin Resolution and passed the Cooper-Church Amendment, prohibiting the use of troops outside South Vietnam, Nixon continued to bomb Cambodia until 1973. An estimated one hundred thousand peasants died in the bombing, and two million people were left homeless. The suffering and devastation rallied the Cambodian peasantry to Pol Pot and, by assuring his success, set the stage for his "killing fields." Was any of this a crime?

During this period Schwendinger defended the students who had been accused by Law School faculty members of being unprofessional. In one of his classes, this defense employed his thinking about the "definition of crime" debate and, after "word got around," doctoral students who were editors of *Issues in Criminology*, asked him to write an article for their journal.[6]

The challenge to customary limits of professional activity in criminology was picked up. It helped undermine the legitimacy of Bowker and Sindler's insistence that the School had no other purpose beyond serving the state.[7]

---

6 Herman Schwendinger and Julia Schwendinger "Defenders of Order or Guardians of Human Rights?" *Issues in Criminology*, 5 (2) Summer. 1970. Pp. 23–157. Julia was at that time a doctoral student at the School.

7 The Schwendingers' article is still in circulation and can be found in Stuart Henry and Mark M. Lanier's 2001 anthology, *What is Crime? Controversies over the Nature of Crime and What to Do about It*. Latham, Maryland: Rowman & Littlefield Publishers, pp. 65–98.

THE SOCIOLOGISTS OF THE CHAIR

Professional legitimacy was challenged in other disciplines. At the 1968 American Sociology Society Conference, for example, Martin Nicolaus astonished the profession by declaring:

> ... the sociologist who always wears the livery, the suit and tie of his masters – this is the type of sociologist who sets the tone of the profession, and it is this type of sociologist who is nothing more nor less than a house servant in the corporate establishment, a white intellectual Uncle Tom not only for this government and ruling class but for any government and ruling class.

Herman and Julia Schwendinger cite Nicolaus' declaration in *The Sociologists of the Chair: A Radical Analysis of the Formative Years of North American Sociology (1883-1922)*. *The Chair*—a shortened title of this wordy book—strongly criticized the founding fathers of American sociology as well as contemporary sociologists who dominated the field. When Herman Schwendinger's tenure was being decided, this work undermined the possibility of receiving unanimously favorable reviews. Other conditions were also important, but they cannot be assessed until readers are familiar with the book.

The book's cover featured an early 20th century political drawing symbolizing how labor leaders like Eugene Debs had viewed the academy. Entitled, "None So Blind As Those Who Cannot Afford To See," the drawing showed academics averting their eyes or using a book and mortarboard to block the sight of a bloated capitalist whose chariot was being drawn by slaves.

The opening chapters unraveled the standpoints producing the academic response to the class relations. It pointed out that during the formative years of American sociology, sociologists generally subscribed to liberalism, the dominant worldview in capitalist societies.[8] However, this did not mean that there were no differences among them. Furthermore, liberalism itself has changed at each stage of capitalist development. Corresponding broadly to mercantile, industrial and monopoly stages, three major variants of liberalism, namely, classical, laissez-faire and corporate liberalism, have emerged. By the turn of the 20th century, all three had sociological exponents even though corporate liberalism eventually dominated when sociology became an academic discipline.[9]

Corporate liberals argued that without political regulation of economic life, capitalism would be destroyed by class conflicts sparked by gigantic corporations, labor unions and socialist movements. Corporate liberals legitimized social inequality, centralization of capital and American imperialism; nevertheless, they also supported the welfare state. Additional doctrines made this liberal variant viable in the face of changing economic and political realities.

Since *The Chair* focused on the relationships between early sociological ideas and long-term developments, trends in liberal thought were "held constant" and the work of intellectual precursors were examined only when they affected these trends. Consequently, it depart-

---

8 *The Chair* broke with histories of sociology that emphasized the influence of Protestantism; it considered liberalism far more important for understanding developments in sociology.

9 These stages are founded on development of mercantile, industrial and monopoly capitalism.

ed significantly from accounts based on the succession of "great men" and a linear approach to the history of social thought. *The Chair*'s discussion of historical precursors of corporate liberalism instead emphasized a highly varied population because, at each new stage of development, intellectuals living during that stage reconstituted the standards influencing the selection and integration of preexisting ideas into liberal thought. For instance, 19th century laissez-faire liberals felt that the French physiocrats had contributed to the doctrine of free trade even though the physiocrats had focused on agrarian rather than an industrial free trade policy. Corporate liberals used Comte's ideas to fashion their own liberal doctrines even though he had been antagonistic to many liberal ideas during his own lifetime. Accordingly, the identification of a person's contribution to liberalism was based first and foremost on an examination of the general contents of liberalism, and not on the writings of any single individual.

Furthermore, for understanding dominant trends, departures from these trends during an individual's career were considered irrelevant. W.I.Thomas changed his mind about the biological basis for female inferiority. When Social Darwinism had dominated sociology, however, his belief in the inferiority of women was clearly evident.

Also, *The Chair* proposed that any attempt to explain the development of sociology in the United States must take into account the university as a prime generator of liberal ideology. Liberalism, in this view, does not merely function as an influential external source of sociological ideas. Academic life is organized generally around liberal precepts, and academics, among others, make liberalism what it is.

C. Wright Mills in "The Professional Ideology of Social Pathologists," had challenged the authority of liberalism among sociologists.[10] He said, "Liberalism has become less of a reform movement than the administration of social services in a welfare state; sociology has lost its reforming push; its tendencies toward fragmentary problems and scattered causation has been conservatively turned to the use of corporation, army and state." Instead of conducting a critical analysis of the political framework of American capitalism, early sociologists at the University of Chicago and elsewhere had identified themselves with law or administration and perceived the everyday troubles of men and women from a bureaucratic point of view. In *The Chair* these sociologists were called "technocrats" or "technocratic scholars" because they instituted administrative and scientific technologies so as to maintain the institutional and class structures that make modern capitalism what it is.[11]

To repel the political unrest and egalitarian movements of the Sixties, sociologists initiated the fashion of calling for renewing faith in the icons of their profession.[12] In 1970, for example, when anti-war protests had escalated, the presidential address to the American Sociological Association by UCB sociologist, Reinhard Bendix safeguarded the noble spirit of "independent inquiry, free discussion and academic self-government"

10 C. Wright Mills. The Professional Ideology of Social Pathologists. *American Journal of Sociology* 49 No.2 Sept. 1943.

11 In state-socialist societies, *The Chair* added, the technocrat performs an analogous role by either stimulating new class differentiations or maintaining the old, under the control of a political oligarchy. (See p152-154)

12 Bloom is another eminent scholar exemplifying this fashion albeit in the humanities.

against the "distrust of reason" exhibited by radical students. Bendix urged sociologists not to heed these barbaric students and abandon the scholarly heritage created earlier by such men as Sigmund Freud, Emile Durkheim and Max Weber.

But what kind of theories and policies did these icons actually create in the name of reason and rationality? According to *The Chair*, Durkheim underwrote an official morality based on technocratic and imperialist doctrines; Freud's theories buttressed the exploitative and sexist conditions in modern societies with the force of natural law; and Weber, despite his qualifications, espoused an elitist doctrine of ideological neutrality.

The Schwendingers also challenged the scientific worth of these icons. For example, they scrutinized Durkheim's *Division of Labor In Society*, considered a classic by technocratic sociologists. However, after comparing this work to Marx's analysis of division of labor under capitalism, *The Chair* concluded that Durkheim's work was decidedly inferior. Aside from its commonsensical interpretations, it was based on a flawed, utopian, utterly classless, syndicalist model of capitalist societies.[13]

Pushing the limit still further, the Schwendingers took on Freud. They found that his patriarchal and homophobic instinct theory was being discredited along with other instinct theories as early as the 1920s in light of L.L. Bernard's discovery of 15,789 separate instincts listed in biological and social-science literature.[14] They noted that

13 Empirical research has falsified Durkheim's theory of retributive and restitutive law.

14 This rejection, of course, preceded the contemporary assault on Freud's approach to homosexuality, gender relations, Oedipal complex, patriarchal family or dreaming and unconscious

founding sociologists had revitalized Freud's pathology of criminal behavior and wrongly attributed the behavior of revolutionaries, labor leaders and homosexuals as "sublimated" deviant adaptations to "disorganized" conditions—by substituting "wishes," "needs" or "values" for instincts.[15]

Finally, specialists in religion and economics have long regarded Weber's theory of the origins of capitalism as untenable. Only in sociology can one find people who continue to believe that his theory has scientific merit.[16]

Unlike Theda Skocpol who claimed that federal support for widows and orphans after the civil war gave birth to the welfare state,[17] *The Chair* contended the welfare state was produced by economic and political conditions occurring in due course among industrial nations. It observed that the founders of American sociology reconstituted liberalism to interpret and deal with class

---

processes, conducted by behavioral, cognitive and neuropsychological research. See, for instance, E. Fuller Torrey's survey, *Freudian Fraud: The Malignant Effect of Freud's Theory on American Thought and Culture*. New York: Harper Collins, 1992.

15 See, for example, the section, The Construction of the Freud-Thomas Bridge in the Chair.

16 Richard F. Hamilton identified twelve empirical claims by Weber. After comparing these claims with historical data, he found (1996: 85–86)) that none of them received unqualified support. (Eight were totally unsupported while confirmation for the remaining claims was ambiguous.) Finally, Hamilton (1996: 91–97), examined citation indices and discovered that Weber's thesis was still being regarded positively by sociological textbooks and eminent sociologists like UCB's Neil Smelser.

17 Theda Skocpol. 1992. *Protecting Soldiers and Mothers: The Political Origins of Social Policy in the United States*, Belknap Cambridge: Harvard University Press.

conflict, political unrest and industrial warfare. Since some of them had been educated in German universities, they knew that German corporate liberals had successfully advised Chancellor Bismarck to stop his futile attempt to crush the Social Democratic Labor Party by force and, instead, to defuse working class discontent by co-opting portions of the socialist party's platform. Adopting their advice, Bismarck got the Reichstag to provide for accident and sickness insurance for workers, old-age insurance ("social security"), industrial sanitation and safety, progressive taxation, protection for women and children, and nationalization of the communication and transportation industries. Such measures, the Schwendingers proposed, successfully challenged the policies of laissez-faire liberalism and created the first "welfare state."[18]

Besides, even though they were corporate liberals, the Germans were called "socialists of the chair" (*Kathedersozialisten*) or "professorial socialists" because they occupied academic "chairs" and because conservatives identified their welfare state policies with "creeping socialism." The Schwendingers adapted the title *Sociologists of the Chair* from this German usage. The title emphasized that American sociology has been essentially an academic enterprise.

While demystifying the icons of American sociology, *The Chair* spelled out its own approach to their writings. It pointed out that their theoretical ideas did not suddenly emerge fully developed because they were being adjusted to rapidly changing conditions. When they searched the past for suggestive ideas to solutions of

---

18 United States was one of the last highly industrial nations to adopt welfare state policies. And it did most of this adoption during the Great Depression, a period of intense class conflict.

new problems, old categories and phrases were used in new ways. Consequently, their theories were at first expressed by "transitional categories" incorporating both new and old ways of thinking. In time, however, the sociological thought born in this process increasingly lost its transitional characteristics. As economic and political changes were being consolidated, they were, so to speak, "rationalized," that is, articulated by formal categories and incorporated into "grand theories" about the nature of man, woman and society. About four decades transpired before these extremely abstract conceptions fully emerged in American sociology.[19]

The Chair also indicated that the founding sociologists rewrote history in a double sense. First, while formulating new conceptions of social evolution, they made their own history by reconstructing the way the past was perceived. They also made history by contributing to ideological perspectives that impinged upon the changing shape of capitalism. Racist doctrines used by American sociologists, for instance, interacted with exploitative relations that differentiated metropolitan from "underdeveloped" countries in Asia, Africa, and South America. They also interacted with the oppression of racial and national groups within the United States. To dramatize the proper context for evaluating their theories, *The Chair* described the robbery, brigandage and genocidal acts generated by American imperialists because they provided an historical background against which the works of the founding sociologists should be

---

19 These developments, of course, did not occur in an ideological vacuum. Between 1880 and 1920, in particular, diverse scholars representing numerous fields throughout the Western world generated the new liberal philosophy of life that eventually led to the construction of new families of ethical, epistemological, and theoretical models of man, woman and society.

evaluated.

For example, Lester Ward, one of the founders of American sociology, claimed that the Bureau of Indian Affairs had treated the Indians equitably. He asserted that a "Negro" who rapes a white woman is not only driven by lust; he is also motivated by a desire "to raise his race to a little higher level." Edward R. Ross, another founder, slandered people in China, India, Africa, and elsewhere. He believed that Jews constituted a distinct race and indicated that the Jews of Eastern Europe, in particular, are "moral cripples, their souls warped and dwarfed." Franklin H. Giddings, another founder, attacked people who opposed the Spanish-American War, exclaiming that the "racial energies" of Anglo-Saxon Americans might discharge themselves in anarchistic, socialistic and other "destructive modes" of life if they were not displaced by imperialist ventures. Charles H. Cooley referred to the feelings of self, which not only distinguished the individual from others, but also the Anglo-Saxon race from its inferiors.[20]

It is also important to note Giddings' justifications for American imperialism. They castigated anti-imperialists for ignoring the "cosmic laws" about "the survival of the fittest" which had been popularized by the great champion of laissez-faire liberalism, Herbert Spencer. Never-

---

20 He observed that "controlled by intellect and purpose, this passion for differentiation becomes self-reliance, self-discipline, and immutable persistence in private aim: qualities which more than any others make the greater power of superior persons and races." Comparing Northern Europeans to Southern Europeans, Cooley further wrote that the former, "less given to blind enthusiasm for popular idols have more constructive power in building ideals from various personal sources . . . [they] are more sober and independent in their judgment of particular persons . . . their idealism is all the more potent. . ." etc.

theless, Giddings revised Spencer's social Darwinism to suit his own political stance. Although he rejected Spencer's laissez-faire opposition to gunboat colonial policies, he kept the faith with Spencer's racism. The same was true of other founders such as Ward, Ross, and Cooley.

As social Darwinism was being discarded, reform Darwinism emerged as a transitional school of thought.[21] Ward, Giddings, Ross, and Cooley modified Spencer's social Darwinism because they believed that social reformers, public administrators and legislators were capable of achieving "enlightened" control of evolutionary social processes. Consequently, in this process, Spencer's "scientific laws" were ripped from their laissez-faire contexts and used to justify reformist liberal doctrines. By modifying his racist, environmentalist and evolutionary "laws" so that they could justify "guided" social change,[22] social reformers could adopt a number of Spencer's Darwinist assumptions to justify accelerating evolutionary changes, in an "enlightened" manner.[23]

The Chair further demystified the founders, showing that some of their writings proposed public policies that would ameliorate gender inequality. But Ward and Thomas, for instance, filtered their proposals through the belief that female intelligence had deteriorated biologically, even though they agreed with Lewis Henry Mor-

---

21 This phrase was borrowed from Richard Hofstadter (*Social Darwinism in American Thought*. New York: George Braziller 1959).

22 After all, Spencer also believed reformers were quite capable of introducing social changes, even though legislation aimed at prolonging the lives of "degenerate races" would be disastrous for the human species.

23 Simultaneously, his "structural and functional" analytic strategy was also modified to serve these ends.

gan that prehistoric women were born superior or equal to men. Women, in their view, had become inferior because they had to adapt biologically to bland environmental conditions created by their passive nature or by restrictions imposed by males who were more aggressive and sexually motivated. To enhance the gradual evolution of female intelligence, these reform Darwinists supported stimulating educational environments for women. Nevertheless, underlying their support was the assumption that females were in fact biological inferiors.[24]

Furthermore, *The Chair* noted that reform Darwinism shaped liberal explanations of other kinds of social inequality. Ross, the granddaddy of social-control theory, for instance, considered his work a scientific guide to social problems like crime and political unrest. He believed in the superiority of the "Aryan race." He asserted that Aryan superior intelligence, enterprise and daring posed special problems for officials, executives and educators. Unlike unintelligent, slothful and cowardly Africans and Asians, the Aryans could not be controlled by force, superstition and religion alone. Therefore, he

---

24 Mary Jo Deegan (*Jane Addams and the Men of the Chicago School*, 1892–1918, New Brunswick: Transaction Books, 1988) objects that the Schwendingers ignored Thomas' later writings, which oppose biological determination of female inequality. However, Thomas' later writings were in this context irrelevant because the object of analysis was 'transitional theories' and dominant ideologies. (The Schwendingers' Introduction plainly indicates the epistemological grounds for differentiating theoretical trends and ideologies from individuals.) Deegan also ignores their discussion of the word 'radical.' She believes that a Fabian socialist is necessarily a radical even though socialist ideas, 'sweetwater socialists' and corporate liberalism were not always mutually exclusive. There was plenty of room for Fabian ideas among the *Kathedersozialisten*.

encouraged people who managed social institutions to adopt "sophisticated" measures that cultivate *self-control* and thereby encourage Aryans to conform voluntarily to the law.

The Chair uncovered still another dimension of corporate liberalism based on liberal syndicalism, a transitional view of social class and class conflict. This form of syndicalism was developed by Albion Small, Durkheim and others who reinvigorated liberalism in the face of growing class war between gigantic corporations, on one hand, and labor and socialist movements on the other.[25] Small's syndicalist writings objected to laissez-faire views of the economy and the state. He defined market relations within the context of society as a whole, and reoriented sociologists toward pluralist theories and doctrines emphasizing class harmony, class collaboration and the "functional interdependence" of economic groups.

Small was particularly important for the formation of academic sociology because he was critical to the emergence of sociology at the University of Chicago. As an administrator, he determined who would be employed in the first sociology graduate program and who would publish articles in the first sociology journal in the United States. *The Chair* exposed the class bias and corporate leanings that permeated Small's writings and administrative practices. For example, on several occa-

---

25 While reformulating liberalism, the Americans selected preexisting ideas, whether espoused by liberals or not, that seemed relevant to their analyses of contemporary events. *The Chair* had to describe these ideas and show why they were important. Unfortunately, it pedantically devoted 160 opening pages to various precursors even though their relevance could not be appreciated until transitional theories, bridging the corporate phase of liberalism with earlier phases, were described.

sions, state and federal troops readily supported capital in its war against labor.[26] During Small's tenure, President Cleveland in 1894 dispatched 10,000 infantry, cavalry, and artillery troops to Chicago, the largest U.S. railway center, to suppress striking workers who had crippled engines, overturned freight cars, and sabotaged tracks in the Great Pullman Strike. Corporate barons, some of whom controlled the University of Chicago, had lost millions.[27] Consequently, Small obeyed corporate interests by backing the firing of a University of Chicago faculty member, Edward W. Bemis who, despite his generally critical stand toward the strike, had taken the side of labor.

The Schwendingers also deconstructed Park and Burgess's renowned theory about "universal processes of social interaction." They uncovered the analytic structure of this theory and showed that its explanation of these processes actually did not constitute a theory. It was merely composed of loosely connected formal "metatheoretical abstractions" whose meanings were keyed to "families of theories" formulated by social Darwinists, reform Darwinists, pluralists, psychoanalytic sociologists, and so on.[28]

---

26 Virtual civil war broke out in 1914 when company thugs and state militia in 1914 massacred women and children at Ludlow miner's camp. Enraged detachments of United Mine Workers roamed throughout Colorado after this incident occurred, battling company police and state troopers and dynamiting mine and smelter works owned by John D. Rockefeller. President Wilson at Rockefeller's urging sent thousands of federal troops to Colorado to crush the uprising.

27 A few months after the strike was crushed, the regular army was raised to 50,000 men and more armories were being started in Chicago, New York, and elsewhere, to keep down any possible labor uprising in the future.

28 For the utopian research program underlying these "universal

Furthermore, *The Chair* recognized Park's role in catalyzing the Chicago School of urban sociology. The authors used Harvey W. Zorbaugh's *Gold Coast and the Slum*, which epitomized this school, as still another example of "the professional ideology of social pathology."[29] Examining Zorbaugh's work, *The Chair* found that he caricatured Chicago working-class districts as "disorganized slums" compared to the cohesive upper-class districts in the "Gold Coast." *The Chair* said that Zorbaugh's study was little more than pseudo-scientific apologetics for upper-class control of city life.[30] After examining other works, *The Chair* concluded that Park and Burgess' liberal functionalism, and its major component, "structural functionalism," dominated sociology until the tumultuous 1960s because they served corporate interests in particular, and obfuscated or justified capitalism and its social inequalities in general.

In contrast with the apologetics of sociology's founders, *The Chair* found that free-lance intellectuals early in the 20th century were adding a distinctly different voice to rising urban discontent. Indignantly labeled "muckrakers" (by Theodore Roosevelt), journalists began to publish systematic exposures of corrupt political machines, land frauds, and harmful practices in the food and drug industries. They centered their fire on fraudulent stock-market manipulations by finance capitalists.

---

processes" see *The Chair*'s chapters on Park and Burgess, and Thrasher.

29 Zorbaugh's work is considered a major achievement in Chicago School's development.

30 Zorbaugh indicated that working-class Chicago communities were incapable of running Chicago because they were socially disorganized. The North side, "Gold Coast," composed of upper class families, on the other hand, was deemed entitled to rule because of their superior solidarity and social organization.

These writers excoriated the "public be damned" attitude of the industrial robber barons, and raked the monopolies and monopoly trusts with their scathing criticism.

Simultaneously, such authors as Theodore Dreiser and Jack London began to publish compelling descriptions of the lives of working people. A notable work of this kind was Jack London's *People of the Abyss*. Dressing himself in clothing befitting an unemployed "down-and-out" workingman in London, England, he lived among the people who desperately searched for work but could find no steady employment. From his sensitive observations of interpersonal relations and by noting personal conversations, London illustrated the degree to which "the people of the abyss" aided each other despite the extraordinary deprivation confronting their everyday existence. His ethnographic observations revealed the compassionate and human qualities of the persons he met, as well as the degree to which their spirits were perpetually menaced by poverty.

Although some of London's works were deeply flawed by the racist and social Darwinist attitudes so prevalent among West Coast writers and workers (as well as sociologists), *The People of the Abyss* was a powerful indictment of "the managing class" which oppressed the working people of England. In order to make this indictment, London contrasted this managing class with the Inuit tribe living along the banks of the Yukon River. He regarded the Inuit as an example of "savage folk" who shared their food, shelter, and clothing with each other no matter how little they possessed. London argued that the social organization among these people was superior to modern civilization. He stated, for example, that the Inuit had "their times of plenty and times of famine. In good times they feast; in bad times they die of starvation. But starvation as a chronic condition, present with a large number of them all the time, is a thing unknown." On the other hand, he pointed out, in England the food eaten by "the managing class" as well as "the wine it drinks, the shows it makes, and the fine clothes it wears, are challenged by eight million mouths which have never enough to feed them, and by twice the eight million bodies which have never been sufficiently clothed and housed."

London used what sociologists call "participant-observation" methods to arrive at an understanding of human relations and he succeeded in producing an outstanding ethnographic work. But *The People of the Abyss* never received any credit in professional histories of urban ethnography in the United States. Perhaps the reasons include the fact that London was a nonprofessional who became a socialist around 1905. Perhaps they involve London's belief that social reformers and intellectual "savants" who descended upon slum areas with their "college settlements, missions, charities and what not," were failures. He believed, despite their sincerity, "They do not understand the simple sociology of Christ, yet they come to the miserable and the despised with the pomp of social redeemers." He pointed out that, in spite of their perseverance, they accomplished absolutely nothing "beyond relieving an infinitesimal fraction of the misery and collecting a certain amount of data which might otherwise have been more scientifically and less expensively collected ..." "As someone has said," London caustically concluded, "they do everything for the poor except get off their backs."

Corporate liberalism would never have dominated social thought in the United States without the control exerted by corporations on universities. To demonstrate this control, *The Chair* reviewed Thorsten Veblen's 1918 critical work, *On the Higher Learning*, which used the University of Chicago as a model. Veblen flatly stated that business domination of governing boards had virtually transformed major universities into industrial organizations and their faculties into apologists for finance capital.[31] Upton Sinclair's scathing 1922 book, *The Goose-Step*, went even further. It described the systematic repression of radicals and caricatured as docile geese self-policing academics, heads capped by mortarboards, goose-stepping in military formation at Columbia, Harvard, Pennsylvania, Yale and Chicago universities. It noted that the trustees in leading California universities, including UCB, formed interlocking networks of bankers, corporate directors and attorneys.[32]

At that time, the repressive conditions sustained by this control were indisputable. Political dissidents among the faculty were easily dismissed from employment. Furthermore, dismissal was extremely serious, since there was an academic blacklist in existence. With regard to this, Veblen declared:

> So well is the academic blacklist understood, indeed, and so sensitive and trustworthy is the fearsome loyalty of the common run among academic men, that very few among them will venture openly to say a good word for any one of their colleagues who may have fallen under the displeasure of some incumbent of executive office. This work of intimidation and

---

31 Veblen used, as indicated in *The Chair*, the University of Chicago as a model.

32 Upton Sinclair, *The Goose-Step: a Study of American Education.* Albert & Charles Boni, 1922 Revised Edition. (Orig. 1936)

> subordination may fairly be said to have acquired the force of an institution, and to need no current surveillance or effort.[33]

The Chair described the extent of repression in American universities. It emphasized characteristics of classic academic-freedom cases being ignored by liberal sociologists. For example, Ross was fired after making a racist speech in support of the Asian Exclusion Acts, at a San Francisco labor meeting. He had criticized Leland Stanford, the robber baron who founded Stanford University, for hiring Chinese "coolies" at wages that undermined the living standards of white workers. But Ross was not fired because he was a virulent racist. If he had not criticized Stanford but merely said that Chinese should not be allowed to immigrate to the U.S. or should be denied employment if they did, he would never have been fired.

Another famous case involved the esteemed political economist, Richard T. Ely who had helped Ross find employment after he had been dismissed. Ely had been accused of teaching Marxism at the University of Wisconsin and of sheltering a labor leader during a strike. The university trustees decided the charges were grave enough to examine the truthfulness of the allegations. At their formal hearings, evidence—including testimony from Ely's students showed that he was teaching Marxism only to condemn it; that he informed students about socialism but believed it was destructive; and that he had never entertained a union leader at his home or encouraged workers to strike. Ely, in fact, wrote, if the charges were actually true they would "unquestionably unfit me to occupy a responsible position as an instructor of youth in a great university."

---

33 See *The Chair*, p. 515.

Ely and his defenders impressed the trustees. They did not fire him. However, observing that he would certainly have been fired if he had been a Marxist or supported the strike, *The Chair* concluded that academic freedom couldn't be taken at face value when its *operating* interpretations were being determined by corporate control of universities.

Examination of additional cases involving academics who opposed participation in World War I, like Scott Nearing, showed that universities had room for corporate sycophants, racists and imperialists but they barely tolerated people who militantly supported racial equality, labor unions, socialist parties, anti-war movements or Marxism. Universalistic declarations, however, masked these operating limits of academic freedom. For instance, when the Wisconsin trustees published their decision in the Ely case, which was subsequently inscribed on a tablet in Bascom Hall, they declared,

> In all lines of academic investigation it is the utmost importance that the investigator should be absolutely free to follow the indications of truth wherever they may lead. Whatever may be the limitations which trammel inquiry elsewhere we believe that the great State University of Wisconsin should ever encourage that continual and fearless sifting and winnowing by which alone truth can be found.

After noting the history of academic repression in America, *The Chair* refuted the myth that academics were free to engage in the "fearless sifting and winnowing by which truth alone can be found."

Comparisons with their contemporaries enabled *The*

Chair to also question whether racist, classist and sexist biases were found in the writings of Ward, Ross, Small, Ellwood, Ogburn, Chapin, Park, Burgess, Weatherly and the others simply because they were "men of their time"—mere passive recipients of dominant thinking. Their works were not compared to the works of Marxists alone. Contrasts were made with writings by people like the anarchist William Haywood, the labor leader Eugene V. Debs, and the militant liberal William E.B. Du Bois, who epitomized authentically radical American traditions.[34] Haywood attacked the "race prejudice" expressed by socialists influenced by social Darwinism. Unlike Small's utopian version of liberal syndicalism, he advocated anarcho-syndicalism. In addition to denouncing racism in the American labor movement, Debs condemned American universities for "doing nothing" about the "great labor problem in America" because they got their "money from the other side."[35]

Du Bois reported that he had trouble at Atlanta University because the university could not obtain research funds from wealthy Northern capitalists as long as he remained there.[36] Du Bois had opposed the "Tuskegee Machine" headed by Booker T. Washington that in his opinion placed greater priority on vocational training to provide cheap labor for Northern capitalists than on fighting for Negro suffrage. In his first decade at Atlanta, Du Bois had hoped to establish "a center of sociological research, in close connection and cooperation with Harvard, Columbia, Johns Hopkins and the University of

34 The word "radical" was not confined to Marxian socialist traditions.

35 Debs attributed the source of this remark to University of Chicago President Harper.

36 Du Bois was a liberal at that time but eventually became a socialist.

Pennsylvania." Obviously, since he was a sociologist, this plan was dependent on close and congenial relations with leading members of his profession. His candid remarks at the second annual sociological conference, however, revealed growing disillusionment that these relations would ever be established:

> When we at Atlanta University say that we are the only institution in the US that is making any serious study of the race problem in the US, we make no great boast because it is not that we are doing so much, but rather that the rest of the nation is doing nothing, and we can get from the rest of the nation very little encouragement, cooperation, or help in this work.

Du Bois' autobiography implicates the political dynamics that isolated him from people like Ward, Ross, Small, Ellwood, Ogburn, Chapin, Park, Burgess, Weatherly and the other liberals who became presidents of the American Sociological Society. His career demonstrates that whoever controls the academic labor force also determines the dominant political compositions of professional associations and their publications. Du Bois was forced to leave Atlanta while Robert E. Park, who had been employed for a while as Booker T. Washington's personal secretary and ghostwriter,[37] went on to become a leading academic authority on race relations. Du Bois, some of whose finest works were written while he engaged in political activity following his departure, had to abandon his dream of using social science to change the status of African-Americans in the United States.

---

37 See David Levering Lewis, *W.E.B. Du Bois: A Biography of Race 1868–1919*. New York: Henry Holt & Co. 1993. The term "ghostwriter" is Levering's.

9 | "Reading" the Text

W hen *The Chair* was published, David Matza allowed Basic Books to print a testimonial on the jacket. He called *The Chair* "a brilliant Marxian consideration of the foundations of American sociological theory that will be quite controversial since the Schwendingers take on just about everyone in the field."

The word, "controversial," was an understatement. Two unequivocally polarized reviews of the book appeared in *Contemporary Sociology,* the American Sociological Society book-review journal. The chief editor reported having solicited reviews from two other people; but one could not send a review while the other responded with a 100-page manuscript, far exceeding acceptable page limits. The editor then took an unprecedented step by publishing two unsolicited reviews, one favorable and the other unfavorable.

Phil Heiple's review pronounced *The Chair* "powerful and convincing." He wrote, "The central assertions of this book have long been common knowledge among radical sociologists but never before has there been such a totalistic and fully documented account of the political origins and implications of American sociology." He claimed the work yielded "new insights and reveal hitherto unrealized depths of corporate control over research and education. The extent to which academic scholars are builders and perpetuators of the status quo is indicated with extreme clarity." He applauded the Schwendingers for relying upon Antonio Gramsci's concept of "hegemony" and for classifying Small as an "organic intellectual." He also complimented the Schwendingers for uncovering the transition of sociologists from liberal reformers to technocratic functionaries and the connection between academic repression and the disinterested pursuit of knowledge. Heiple declared, "Much like Baritz's disclosure of the corporate control of industrial psychologists in *The Servants of Power*, the Schwendingers reveal the actual powerlessness of sociologists and the manipulation of sociologists by corporate interests."[1]

The negative review by Peter Kivisto, on the other hand, condemned Schwendinger's assertions. He flatly dismissed their claim that corporate interests controlled universities. He also considered *The Chair*'s moral "indictments" scandalous. Calling American sociology's founders "sexists" and "racists" was especially grating. He rejected the Schwendinger's claim that sociologists had legitimated monopoly capital and formulated technocratic social-control policies.

Kivisto also criticized Schwendinger's treatment of the individuals who had founded sociology.[2] He objected

---

1 Heiple published a second review in *Insurgent Sociologist*. He observed: "The section on academic repression should be mandatory reading for every radical sociologist in the university. It is brilliant, as is the book as a whole."

2 The phrase "organic intellectual" is derived from Gramsci's notebooks written while he was imprisoned by Mussolini. See

to the their depiction of Small as an "organic intellectual" who "muted radical criticism of society." Though he
granted that they employed Gramsci's term "hegemony"
and Lukacs' "reification," he dubbed the Schwendingers
"true positivists" rather than Marxists. Objecting to their
treatment of Durkheim and Freud, Kivisto, on the other
hand, indignantly protested: "[Even] Marx did not engage in such heretical activity; rather, he sought to discover kernels of truth and insight in the work of his
predecessors, working through their tradition rather than
around it."

While Kivisto seemed to have acquired his expertise
from *Marx for Dummies*, Paul J. Baker, another reviewer, must have relied on *Cliff's Evangelical College Notes
on Albion Small*. In a review for the *American Journal
of Sociology,* Baker agreed that the Schwendingers were
heretics. He called *The Chair* "demonology."[3] It was "a
propaganda piece for sectarian socialists but difficult to
take seriously as a work of scholarship." To justify his
allegations, he said the Schwendingers were ignorant of
the facts when they claimed the standards for professional competence by the end of the formative years had become thoroughly "positivistic" (i.e., more precisely, and
perversely, "technocratic"). He insisted that Small "never 'rejected' his own ethical ideas as old fashioned and
opinionated." Furthermore, in his opinion, "there is no
record of pioneer sociologists converting to positivism,
grudgingly or otherwise."

Baker was wrong. *The Chair* had repeatedly demon-

Antonio Gramsci. 1971. *Selections from the Prison Notebooks*.
(editors and translators, Q. Hoare and G. N. Smith) New York:
International Publishers.

3 Paul J. Baker, 1975, "Review of Sociologists of the Chair."
American Journal of Sociology 80 (May) 1487–1489.

strated this conversion. Furthermore, it included the eminent "Christian Sociologist," Albion Small, whose later writings emphasized the newer analytic (i.e., positivistic) methods and minimized those based on a Christian ethic. After making a confession about his own place among the early sociological "sinners," and after castigating sociologists and non-sociologists for their unscientific and naive writings, Small categorically stated, "In short, a humiliating proportion of the so-called 'sociology' of the last thirty years in America ... has been simply old-fashioned opinionativeness under a new-fangled name."[4]

Edward L. Suntrup, in *THE ANNALS*, gave *The Chair* its due. He emphasized *The Chair*'s worthwhileness despite its troubling character: "For those who practice, or pretend to practice value-free science as sociologists, the reading of this book will or should be disturbing. Whether it will be ultimately disturbing will depend upon whether one accepts the authors' historical interpretations and theoretical linkages – and there are many – as well as whether one agrees with their anti-liberalism, Marxist assumptions. In either case, the book is worth reading."[5]

Gale Omvedt, in *Issues in Criminology*, emphasized *The Chair*'s relevance for a feminist approach to sociology.[6] She said, "Giving form to the content and style of their book is the uniqueness of their starting points."

---

4 Albion Small, *Origins of Sociology*, Chicago: University of Chicago Press. 1924, p. 379.

5 Edward L. Suntrup. 1974. *THE ANNALS of the American Academy of Political and Social Science* 416 (November) 257–258.

6 Gail Omvedt, 1973, "Prolegomena To A Feminist Sociology," *Issues in Criminology* 8 (Fall) 163–174.

These included the premise that "equality and freedom from exploitation be the criteria by which a society is judged" and that "equality is possible since inequality and exploitation are not due to 'human nature' or universal 'functional imperatives' of a society." In Omvedt's opinion, *"The Sociologists of the Chair* represents a major challenge to the conventional history of American sociology that would not, like Gouldner's work, be acceptable to the established profession."

Alvin Gouldner had written an admirable book, but he wrongly believed that social theory was moving toward a rapprochement between Marxist and functional sociologies. He claimed a critical sociology would emerge from reflexive awareness of value commitments on the part of individual scientists. Yet, this claim overrated individualistic and subjective criteria for scientific knowledge and it underestimated the effect of material conditions on theoretical preferences. *The Chair,* among other things, urged radical sociologists to counter these conditions by supporting their own associations, journals, conferences and other joint activities to compensate for the isolation most feel in their departments.

The radical movement at the Criminology School influenced the Schwendingers. But their work was not governed by a knee-jerk accord with the movement's ethical or political imperatives. Certainly, commitments to egalitarian ideals influenced their work; but the reviews that denounced them for "finding what they were looking for" had dismissed an elemental criterion for judging research. They had found what they were looking for because their study, at every turn, *confirmed* theoretical ideas proposed by C. Wright Mills, Dusky Lee Smith, James Weinstein and William Appleman

Williams.[7]

Ironically, the research producing *The Chair* did not originally aim at an historical analysis of sociology's founders. At first, the Schwendingers were merely interested in background material for introducing their book on subcultures and delinquency. Their own field observations and interviews had invalidated and rejected highly praised delinquency theories by Albert Cohen, Richard Cloward and Lloyd Ohlin, who followed in Robert K. Merton's footsteps.[8] (Regardless, even though their delinquent subcultures were fictitious entities, Cohen's *Delinquent Boys* and Cloward and Ohlin's *Delinquency and Opportunity*, were cited 1,145 times—more citations than any other basic theoretical work on delinquency published from 1945 to 1972!) How could these predecessors provide reliable traditions? Skepticism and cynicism were more appropriate.

Besides, Schwendingers' search for empirical studies backing August Hollingshead's theory encouraged further disenchantment. Sociologists in the Fifties and Sixties were positively convinced that August Hollingshead had produced the definitive work on social class and

---

7   C. Wright Mills, 1949, "The Professional Ideology of Social Pathologists." *American Journal of Sociology* 49 (September) 165–180. Dusky Lee Smith, 1965, "Sociology and the Rise of Corporate Capitalism." *Science and Society* 29 (Fall) 401–418. James Weinstein, 1968, *The Corporate Ideal and the Liberal State: 1900–1918*. Boston: Beacon Press. William Appleman Williams, 1961, *The Contours of American History.* New York: World.

8   Albert Cohen, 1955, *Delinquent Boys, The Culture of the Gang.* Glencoe, Ill.: Free Press. Richard Cloward and Lloyd Ohlin, 1960. *Delinquency and Opportunity*. Glencoe, Ill.: Free Press. Robert K. Merton, 1938, "Social Structure and Anomie." *American Sociological Review* 3 (October) 672–682.

peer relations.[9] How could this be? *Every single large-s-cale sociometric study uncovered by the Schwendingers disconfirmed his thesis.* Furthermore, theoretical alternatives to Hollingshead's structural functional theory of social class and peer relations were virtually nonexistent. To discover what accounted for this disgraceful state of affairs, the Schwendingers turned back to earlier periods in the development of sociology. What was the result?

By the end of the Sixties, Schwendinger had been encouraged by Herbert Blumer, an outstanding sociologist, to publish his dissertation. But Herman's obsessive quest for understanding what went wrong with delinquency theory had taken on a life of its own. He systematically detected links that connected Merton's and Hollingshead's classic works to the founders of American sociology. This exploration finally involved his wife, Julia, who had been a co-director in a research project on delinquency funded by the NIMH. Working together, they ignored the possibility that Herman's tenure at Berkeley would have been secured by the publication of his dissertation. Instead they single-mindedly pursued the origins of delinquency theories about delinquency.

They knew that sociology in their time was dominated by what was called "structural functionalist theories." But, they tried to understand why American sociologists believed structural functional theories were true. Robert Merton's "general theory of deviance," for instance, was contradicted by every crime committed by powerful and wealthy people. Moreover, they realized that delinquency subculture theories—despite the existence of delinquency committed by children of well-to-do families—were also dependent for their credibility on com-

---

9 August B. Hollingshead, 1949, *Elmtown's Youth*. New York: John Wiley.

mon-sense wisdom backed by centuries-old observations about street crimes and economic disadvantage?

How can theories that produce no genuinely new information about human relationships be considered major contributions to science? Competent scientists automatically raised questions like these, but they seemed stuck in the throats of structural functionalists so they couldn't spit them out.

To identify the ideological functions of sociological writings, the Schwendingers' analytic usage of "sexism," "racism," "imperialism" and "exploitation" conformed to countless other Marxian works that used these categories for classifying theoretical as well as moral standpoints. Ironically, sociologists like Kivisto and Baker denounced realistic concepts like "sexism" and "imperialism" as ideological and not analytic, while concepts like "social control" produced by founding sociologists were regarded as analytic and not ideological.

Kivisto and Baker believed that analytic thinking was unaffected by history and, in this case, by the demands for sexual, racial, national and economic equality being raised by centuries-old social and political movements whose advocates created their own ideas about the possibilities of human existence.

Still, there were more subtle reasons for understanding the response to *The Chair*. Michael T. Ort's review, in *Crime and Social Justice*, revealed these reasons by concentrating on *The Chair*'s epistemology.[10] He said the book had features not duplicated elsewhere. It contained an approach to the "theory of theory" which may

---

10 Michael Ort, 1975, "Social Theory, Ideology and the Technocratic Structure." *Crime and Social Justice* 4 (Fall–Winter) 66–70.

not have been familiar to its readers. Social theory has been studied from the "sociology-of-knowledge" perspective, which situates social thinking within specific socio-historical environments and shows how it arises to pose or solve certain problems. Ort asserted, "This the Schwendingers do but they go much further by exploring the internal logic and tacit assumptions of dominant theories." Because of *The Chair*'s interests in the analytic structures underlying theories, it "never degenerates into either an economically or environmentally deterministic explanation as is so typical of many Marxist and sociological discourses on theoretical topics." He believed that appreciating *The* Chair required a careful reading as well as analytic capability.

Because of *The Chair*'s analytic approach, Ort predicted that "readers will not find either an exposition of theoretical perspectives absolutely adhering to the order of historical development or a discussion of the complete contribution made by each theorist."[11] To clarify this important point, Ort added, "Again, this work is not a simple enumeration of theoretical ideas, but is an analysis of the integral relationship between social structure, ideology, social theory, and the social framework in which it is produced. It is not concerned, for example, with the 'richness' of W. I. Thomas's thought, but only with his contribution to the development of liberalism in social theory." Unfortunately, "it is precisely this analytic approach which has baffled some hackneyed reviewers who looked to the text for a common-place 'history of ideas' or a ponderous exposition of the 'linear' development of 'scientific' knowledge."

The Chair had added problems with hackneyed reviewers because it challenged the idea that the founders

---

11 Ort considers this approach both "structural" and "synchronic".

should merely be considered "waxen tablets" inscribed with the racism of their times. Marx's writings certainly cannot be regarded as the last word on the topic of 19th-century exploitation and imperialism, but they certainly were superior to Herbert Spencer's. If applied creatively and systematically to American conditions, a Marxian analysis would have linked racial and national oppression to capitalist development and imperialism. It certainly would not have interpreted these forms of oppression, as did founders like Ross, in the context of a universal struggle for existence among biologically superior and inferior races.[12]

The book backed this assertion by comparing the founders' works with contemporaneous, alternative ways of thinking. For example, Ward, as indicated, wrote about the subjugation of women. *The Chair* compared his theory to Engels' theory and showed that these men faced similar analytic options and, at least in part, the same theoretical problems. Both of them rejected the prevalent notion that women were slaves of men in the earliest prehistoric times. Each of them, moreover, predicted equality for women in the future. Furthermore, anthropological interest and theories about women, marriage and the family had developed rapidly during the two decades prior to 1883 when Ward's first work dealing with women was published. Although comparative knowledge was still undeveloped, Ward and Engels had

---

12 Their writings reinforced the ideas that had influenced liberals and nonliberals alike. When socialist leaders such as Eugene Debs and William Haywood began to denounce the "race prejudice" which had been expressed by such socialists as Victor Berger, they were struggling against the effects of liberalism. During the formative years, Spencerism, social Darwinism, and neo-Malthusian ideas, rather than Marxian theories, were adopted in writings and policies of many socialists.

available the same assortment of ideas about the evolution of human society. These ideas included: social-Darwinist categories based on natural selection; psychological categories for male aggression such as instinct; technological categories that linked evolutionary developments with economic change; socio-economic categories referring to changing modes of production; and an array of political categories useful for solving the problem of social integration.

As the most plausible keys to the origins of the subjugation of women and the institution of marriage and the family, Ward, oriented toward liberalism, chose man's sexual passion, man's desire for private property, woman's desire for security, and various reductionist mechanisms linked with the concepts of natural selection and scarce resources. Engels, moving in a materialist direction, based the major part of his explanation on changes in the modes of production, private property and origins of the state. Male sexual passions, he insisted, had nothing to do with the origins of the patriarchal family.[13]

The Schwendinger's insisted that the founders of sociology were *relatively* autonomous agents. They rode the initial wave of modern university development, relatively unencumbered by ancient academic traditions. They rapidly institutionalized their status as members of a newly independent discipline within the academy. They established separate sociology departments much earlier than the Europeans, and were able to train a much larger core of professional sociologists who applied the

---

13 Engels said the patriarchal family "was not in any way the fruit of individual sex-love, with which it had nothing whatever to do." See, Frederick Engels, 1968, *The Origin of the Family, Private Property, and the State*. Moscow: Progress Publishers, p.62. Originally published in 1884.

new ways of thinking to greater varieties of social issues. As a consequence, Americans, like Ross, were far
more capable of elaborating the programmatic implications of categories such as "social control" by which social and political hegemony had been, was being, and
could be maintained.

The Chair treated ideological knowledge as the by-
product of complex processes that exhibited an internal
dynamic of their own.[14] For example, although Park and
Burgess formulated their own theories, the uniqueness of
their contribution to functionalist theories lay in their
ability, first, to distinguish distinct trends in social
thought; second, to extract widely used paradigms from
preexisting "families of theories," and third, to parsimo-
niously reconceptualize and formalize these paradigms.[15]
Eventually, what the Schwendingers dubbed the
"metatheoretical formulations" produced by this process
came to be classified by Park and Burgess as "universal
processes of social interaction." *The Chair* identified
these so-called empirical processes as components of a
tacit utopian liberal paradigm that guided future genera-
tions of sociologists. Furthermore, Park and Burgess'
works reinforced the conviction that the corpus of liberal
theories was an objective, *value-free* representation of
reality.

Examples of how this metaphysics worked were described in a chapter devoted to "urban technography"

---

14 This stress on relative autonomy touches on a later debate over
the value of decoupling ideology from social structure in
structural analyses. "In the absence of any degree of autonomy it
becomes impossible to examine their interplay," Margaret Archer
insists.

15 These men were also adept at identifying common analytic
strategies to make them available to other scholars.

(i.e., technocratic urban ethnography). This pioneering approach to social problems was innovated by The Chicago School of ethnography. Under Park's tutelage, for instance, sociologists studied social problems posed by hobos, prostitutes and gangs. While these studies in some cases reflected the humanistic intentions of their authors, their analytic frameworks were grounded in social-control theory and their causal schema were based on opportunities for the gratification of desires.

In *The Hobo*, for instance, Anderson proposed that individuals become tramps and hobos because of unemployment, seasonal work, discrimination, or personal crises and defects. So far, so good. However, once committed to a migratory mode of existence, the hobo hungers for intimate associations and affections, even though he is "disbarred from family life." Therefore, because his "fundamental wishes for response and status have been denied expression," the hobo attempts to realize these wishes by alternative means. But look where Anderson takes us from here. Deprived of sexual fulfillment, the hobo turns to homosexuality. Denied status in organized society, "he longs for a classless society where all inequalities shall be abolished." "In the Industrial Workers of the World and other radical organizations, he finds in association with restless men of his own kind the recognition everywhere else denied him."[16]

Cressey's *The Taxi-Dance Hall* was published ten years after *The Hobo*. By that time, sociologists in this technographic series classified an individual's behavioral regularities according to "cycles" of development. According to Cressey, the first cycle in the taxi dancer began with a working girl's dissatisfaction with the type

---

16 Nels Anderson, *The Hobo*. Chicago: University of Chicago Press. 1923, p. 149.

of life associated with her home and neighborhood. Driven by the frustrated desire for money, masculine contacts, or status, the girl "finds her way to the taxi-dance hall, wherein she is able to secure a satisfaction of certain wishes previously unfulfilled." At the dance hall, the girl finds herself "rushed" and "enjoys the thrill of being very popular." In time, however, she must make "a deliberate effort to maintain her status." If she fails and is no longer able to secure sufficient patronage exclusively from the white group [men], "she comes eventually to accept the romantic attentions of Filipinos and other Orientals." Failure to maintain the prestige accorded by the Orientals results in frequenting the "black and tan" cabarets. If she fails to maintain her prestige in the cabarets, she finally turns to prostitution in the "black belt."

Nowhere in these works do you find causality linked to the evils of a class society. In Anderson's and Cressey's studies we find the repetitive use of Thomas' four "wishes," frustrated striving, and such functionally equivalent relationships as "family life," a socialist labor organization or status relations in white or Asian or "black and tan" dance halls. In later decades, the American Dream (i.e., desires for social status or economic mobility) replaced the four wishes; and functionally equivalent relationships were converted into formal categories by middle-range metatheorists (e.g., "legitimate" and "illegitimate opportunity structures").

In reality, this process of "metatheorizing," of abstracting paradigmatic ideas commonly found in theories and then dubbing these ideas "universal processes" or "middle-range theories" has never been empirically validated in any scientific discipline. Merton's so-called "general theory of deviancy" exemplifies how this unscientific approach was applied in the sociology of "deviancy" and in criminology.

While describing these metatheoretical developments and their accompanying rhetoric of ideological neutrality, *The Chair* urged radical sociologists to move beyond criticism of each liberal category or each liberal theory or each liberal school of thought. It provided an analytic strategy that identified whole families of liberal theories and schools of thought. Unfortunately, using these "families" in research meant the unwitting adoption of the "way things are" from the standpoint of a corporate-liberal metaphysics of normality.

Chapter 8 in *The Chair* noted that C. Wright Mills, in "The Professional Ideology of Social Pathologists," had challenged the authority of liberalism as early as 1959. Left-liberals, anarchists and socialists in the late Sixties greatly expanded Mills' critique. Eventually, their writings shattered the hegemony of structural functional paradigms in sociology and, to a degree, helped broaden the political composition of sociology departments. Simultaneously, however, they created a professional "crisis of legitimacy" that galvanized eminent liberal sociologists in defense of their technocratic discipline.

Looking back to the formative years, for example, eminent sociologists such as Robert Nisbet claimed that liberal scholarship at the turn of the century represented the culmination of a golden age in social thought.[17] Men like Durkheim, Weber, Simmel, Freud, and Tönnies were considered the foremost products of this golden age, and those who followed in their footsteps were, by implication, their scions. *The Chair*, however, suggested

---

17 Robert A. Nisbet, *The Sociological Tradition*. New York: Basic Books. 1966.

that establishment sociology—as an outcome of the most abstract ideas produced during the formative years —has been able to justify social repression in the name of freedom, to color technocratic aims with humanitarian-sounding platitudes, and to mask ideological engagement with the doctrine of ideological neutrality.

Other sociologists like Reinhard Bendix, for example, claimed that the writings of "classical" sociologists at the turn of the century were informed by the traditions of rationalism and romanticism, which had emerged in the 18th and 19th centuries. But *The Chair* showed that corporate-liberal works from the formative years were not actually generated by a desire for enlightened accommodation between rationalism and romanticism. These writings represented an intellectual accommodation to social inequality, imperialism and monopoly capitalism. Neither the liberating passions nor the rational optimism that emerged toward the end of the Age of Reason informed European and American corporate liberals at the turn of the 19th century.

The formative years of modern sociology began when the pioneering sociologists in America were preoccupied with the maintenance of capitalism, not its destruction. In their reformist zeal to achieve both order and progress, they condemned the egotistical souls of business barons but declared that conflict between syndicated capital and labor was reconcilable. They illuminated their sociological visions of a capitalist utopia with the shiny faces of efficient people bound together in the mythical solidarity of bygone days. The spirits of Malthus, Comte, and Darwin walked through their pages and even Christ himself was called upon in time of need. For four stormy decades they employed the writings of the quick and the dead to revitalize the universal ideas of

19th century liberalism. By the 1920s, the leading members of the new generation of sociologists had begun to abandon the secular and religious images of benevolent humanitarianism that had justified their conservative reformist tradition. In a climate of political repression, Park, Burgess, Ogburn and others consolidated metatheoretical developments in the field and replaced the liberal rhetoric of benevolence with the liberal technocratic rhetoric of neutrality. The clarion voice of the social reformer was muted. The cautious professional tone of the academic scientist and clean-cut image of the administrative-consultant now stood alone: With the standardization of a formal ensemble of categories and the professionalization of the field, the pioneering phase of sociology came to an end. In 1921 and 1922— at the pinnacle of its early development— a new phase in the history of the field began.

10 | Schwendinger Denied Tenure

A long with Platt's losing battle for tenure and the assassination of the School, Herman Schwendinger
was shot down. Subsequently, Julia Schwendinger and
an ex-Jesuit Dean of Liberal Arts as well as the sociology faculty at the State University of New York, New
Paltz, restored his professional career. Prior to his doctorate in sociology, Schwendinger had earned a Masters
in Social Work from Columbia University. His social
work experience centered on adolescent groups, including street gangs; and when he became a doctoral student
in 1959 at UCLA, he utilized trusted relations with gang
members to jump-start his research on adolescent subcultures and delinquency. By 1963, when he graduated,
he had spent almost four years as "participant observer"
studying Los Angeles gangs.

Shortly before receiving Herman's PhD, the
Schwendingers applied for a half-million-dollar grant to
extend their "instrumental theory" of delinquency.[1]
Since neither Herman nor Julia actually had a doctoral
degree in hand, they needed a sponsor who would assure
the National Institute of Mental Health that the grant

---

1 The grants were among the highest received for research by any
member of the School faculty. They finally totaled over $500,000
when Herman's tenure review occurred.

would be administered responsibly. Joseph Lohman offered to be their sponsor,[2] funneling the grant through the Berkeley School of Criminology, even though the research was conducted in Los Angeles.[3] Their project was partly dependent on well-established contacts with young criminals who were actively engaged in illegal market activities; therefore, it had to be conducted in this southern California city.

When Schwendinger started teaching at Berkeley in 1967, he was known as an innovative researcher. The importance of research methods (for the development of theory and as "instruments of discovery") was instilled in him early at Stuyvesant High School, an exceptional New York City public school devoted to science and engineering.[4] Next, Schwendinger attended another outstanding institution known widely as the "Poor Man's Harvard"—the College of the City of New York, where he was a psychology major.[5] Consequently, instead of merely relying on survey methods or official data, he utilized field observations, small-group field experiments, sociometric procedures and other social-psychological methods seldom used in criminology. To obtain data required by his "instrumental theory," he devel-

---

2 Harold Garfinkel, a brilliant sociologist at UCLA, also had offered to be a sponsor.

3 Julia also had a Masters in Social Work from Columbia and she was enrolled in sociology at UCLA. Her graduate student career in sociology, however, was interrupted by the research project (which she co-directed) and the move to Berkeley. She enrolled in the School's doctoral program and graduated in 1974.

4 Reportedly more Nobel Laureates graduated from Stuyvesant High than any other high school in the world.

5 We've also seen the phrase, "Harvard of the Proletariat," used in a *NY Times* article. Established in the mid-1800s, CCNY was the first free college in the world. And, despite the nickname, it was better than Harvard.

oped, among other things, methods for quantifying sub-cultural identities and sociometric/mathematical proce-dures for analyzing networks composed of thousands of youth.[6]

A manuscript with some of these methods and find-ings had been accepted around 1968 for publication in a Prentice Hall series edited by Herbert Blumer.[7] Howev-er, instead of simply following up editorial suggestions and sending it in, the Schwendingers procrastinated. They wanted to include a macro sociological theory of adolescent subcultures that was not completed until the early 1970s.[8] Also, they were anxious about the potential political abuse of their procedures for mapping large subcultural networks.[9] Delaying publication and com-

---

6 By the late 1970s, co-authored with Julia, his theoretical ideas and experimental work had been published and in some cases republished in professional publications. See also, their discussion of the field methods used for "spot checks." Their 'Galilean' empirical strategy is detailed in "Charting Subcultures at a Frontier of Knowledge." *British Journal of Sociology.* 48 (March) 1977, pp. 71–94. The 1970 article, "Defenders of Order or Guardians of Human Rights" was reprinted in *What is Crime: Controversies over the Nature of Crime and What to do about It,* (eds.) Stuart Henry and Mark M. Lanier. New York: Rowman and Littlefield 2001 pp. 65–98.

7 This manuscript was based on Schwendinger's dissertation.

8 The essentials of this macro theory were published in a 1976 article.

9 Our concern about this possibility was based on our success in using sociometric data (in 1965–1966) to identify large informal networks. Also, see, for instance, the article on grand jury investigations and use of a 'sociogram strategy' for identifying anti-war networks in Frank J. Donner and Eugene Cerruti, "The Grand Jury Network: How the Nixon Administration Has Secretly Perverted A Traditional Safeguard of Individual Rights," *The Nation,* January 3, 1972, pp 5–15, 18–20. See, for a later example, Roger H. Davis, 1981, "Social Network Analysis: An Aid in

pleting their work on *The Chair* finally resolved their uncertainties.

When the first draft of *The Chair* was completed, the Schwendingers circulated it and received encouraging responses. The manuscript was given to Messinger, who had replaced Wilkins as Acting Dean. In a memo to Schwendinger, dated July 7, 1971, he said: "That really is a magnificent book! I have no doubt at all about its publishability. I think it will be reviewed appreciatively, if sometimes with anger. You have accomplished a great deal."

He made editorial suggestions and offered to contact Aldine, where he served as an editor of an academic series. The Schwendingers, however, decided to send their manuscript to Basic Books, an eminent publisher, where it was reviewed and accepted for publication.[10] Because of its size, the firm contracted with the Schwendingers to produce a two-volume work. But, after discovering how much both volumes would cost readers, the Schwendingers got the publisher to lower the purchase price by combining the volumes.

The Chair was essential to Schwendinger's quest for tenure. However, since the combined work ran to more than 600 printed pages, the period for processing the publication was prolonged. As a result, only difficult to read, bound photocopies of about 1100 unedited pages of the immense typewritten manuscript were sent by the senior faculty to the three sociologists—Richard Quin-

---

Conspiracy Investigations," FBI Law Enforcement Bulletin, December, pp. 1–9.

10 Basic Books was the only publisher sent the book. After the reviews requested by the School were received and evaluated, the Schwendingers with the help of students reorganized and edited the manuscript. They are forever grateful for this help.

ney, Norman Birnbaum, Lewis Coser—and an anthropologist, Marvin Harris.

Quinney called *The Chair* "a major achievement." He believed the Schwendingers provided "a more critical, more insightful, and more extensive analysis of American sociology" than Gouldner's *Coming Crisis of Western Sociology.*[11] He said *The Chair* destroyed the myth about the origin of sociology as a liberating force. It showed that concepts and theories formulated during the formative years—as a response to social and economic turmoil—still guided the work of many social scientists. Quinney approved of analyses of Ward, Small and Ross' relationship to the social and economic context of their time. He congratulated the Schwendingers for their work.

Coser condemned the book. "I have gone through all four volumes, [12] a feat which, where there's any justice in this dismal world, I should be awarded several Boy Scout stars." He said, "No effort is made to place the figures discussed in the general social and historical context of their time." In fact,

> [The Schwendingers] judge all writings of the past in terms of present Left standards. Hence these men [the founders of American sociology] are accused of racism, sexism, imperialism, etc. while no attempt is made to explain why these men made the statements they made. To be sure few of these men came up to the purity of women's lib. [sic] ideology espoused by the authors,

11 Alvin Gouldner, *Coming Crisis of Western Sociology*, New York: Basic Books, 1970.

12 These typewritten pages were bound in four segments that Coser assumed were four volumes.

> but why should they have, considering the
> context of their culture and their time? To be
> sure, E.A. Ross wrote some sharp things
> against the Chinese, etc. immigrants, but
> there is no indication here that he did this in
> terms of his 'progressive' defense of
> American wage earners and the threat to
> their standard of living by oriental
> immigration. (The point is not that Ross was
> right, it is however that he cannot be
> assessed properly if one doesn't indicate
> why he made the statements he made.)

The Schwendingers, Coser added, are as relentless as a
"D.A. who, through selective use of the evidence, shows
that the accused is guilty—of non radicalism. . . . This is
pamphleteering rather than scholarship." The book, in
his eyes, could not be compared with works by C.
Wright Mills or Alvin Gouldner. He concluded, "I doubt
very much that it will find a publisher and it is my considered opinion that it lacks any redeeming scholarly
value."

Ironically, a contract for the publication of *The Chair*
had been signed before Coser evaluated it. Yet, his comments about Ross were more revealing of his poor judgment. Ross, despite Coser's estimation, did not defend
American wage earners. He defended *white* wage earners. His so-called "progressive" stance rode roughshod
over other racial groups in America; and his theory of
Aryan supremacy included, in addition to Asian immigrants, the Native Americans who were annihilated in
Northern California.[13] Finally, *The Chair* is set apart

13 See, for example, Sherburne F. Cook, *The Conflict Between the
California Indians and White Civilization,* Berkeley: University
of California Press, 1976. Also, Theodora Kroeber, *Ishi in Two
Worlds: A Biography of the Last Wild Indian in North America.*

from other historical works because it exposed the racist content of Ross' defense of working-class living standards. That defense did not take place in a world created by sociological myths. It took place in a real world where other men of Ross' time, Debs and Haywood, knew that racism kept workers divided and more exploitable.[14]

Unlike Coser's, Birnbaum's review was positive even though he emphasized his "reading was hasty, with a great deal of sampling." He found "the effort to reinterpret the early history of American sociology commendable." He also found "it difficult to disagree with the general ideological characterization of the period in the text." While he observed, "the authors have gone to considerable trouble to depict the primary sources," he felt they ignored "one or two important works" and "tended to use stereotypes (e.g., sexism and racism)." Nevertheless, he said the book was "better than a good deal of work on American sociology, and will cause some readers to reflect on matters they hitherto ignored." He felt that it was not a work "in the intellectual class" of Mills or Gouldner. Still, he also felt that "if the level of work found in the authors I have just mentioned were required for tenure, most American academic departments would be emptied, rather rapidly, of their teachers."

Harris's review was irresponsible. He was obviously too busy and should have sent the manuscript back without reviewing it. He believed *The Chair* was a doctoral dissertation and said its organization was "execrable." He said Schwendinger had the worst case of "foot-and-note disease" he has seen. "Most of Schwendinger's evi-

---

Berkeley: University of California Press, 1969.

14 Wage levels among white workers are higher in industries where racial disparities are lower.

dence seems to consist of the analysis of theory—what he calls metatheory. Personally, I find this kind of approach to the harlot functions of academia irredeemably scholastic."

After continuing in this vein, Harris wrote,

> Perhaps, if I could have read the four tomes on an uninterrupted schedule, I would not have soured on them quite so much. (But who has such opportunities?) It would be grossly unfair to give the impression that I was not educated by my experience. I learned a great deal and if I had a copy to consult over the years, I'm sure I would find it very useful. I hope that in a more cogent form it will be published.

Despite Birnbaum's review, the other reviews were baffling or equivocal. (What could be said about a reviewer who complains about organization of *The Chair* and the fact that the author is "irredeemably scholastic?") Consequently, even though Schwendinger teaching evaluations were outstanding, the decision regarding tenure was delayed pending responses from a new set of reviewers.

This delay was justified by Messenger who noted that the School's future was in doubt. He also said that Schwendinger should be spared further anxiety for the moment. Schwendinger, at that time, was having great difficulty coping with Julia's life-threatening bout with cancer.

Schwendinger's bid for tenure obviously was in deep trouble. Realizing this, he wrote to John Horton, respected by left-wing sociologists, for a review which had been written for Basic Books. It was sent to Bowker who added it to the other reviews. Horton had called the work exceptional. He said, "C. Wright Mills perhaps comes closest to the critical spirit of *The Sociologists of the Chair*. Yet the latter is more sweeping in its social analysis. Mills traces connections between professional ideologies and middle class beliefs and institutions. The Schwendingers relate professional ideologies to ruling beliefs and institutions." He said *The Chair* was more accurately historical than Gouldner's effort and more macrosociological than Mills' critique.

Although Schwendinger only had a cursory acquaintance with Immanuel Wallerstein, he also sent him the draft of the book. Wallerstein's pioneering volumes on the modern world system made his national and international stature greater than the reviewers selected in the first and second stages. To make sure he was fully informed, Schwendinger sent copies of the first tenure reviews. He replied, "I'm sorry to have taken so long to write to you. But this has been a busy period and I wanted to read your book carefully. I have now done so." Wallerstein added,

> It is a very good book indeed, and I am very glad you asked me to read it. It shows very clearly what you say it does—the socio-intellectual roots of contemporary American sociological theory in the transformation of the U.S. and world economic structures around the turn of the 20th century. You show how the now largely unread early American sociologists (Ward, Small, et al) reflected the need to cope ideologically with the changed social situation. This is of course what one would expect, but you spell

it out. What is even more striking is the
degree to which the ideas of the post-second
World War era are continuous with the
earlier ideas. This challenges the
conventional history of the discipline, which
you and I were taught as graduate students,
to wit, that Parsons' Structure of Social
Action revolutionized thinking in U.S.
sociology. It turns out that what he really did
is to show Americans that the ideas they
were using had really been stated earlier in
similar, if in perhaps more sophisticated,
terms by European scholars.

Wallerstein indicated the style of the book presented a
problem. He said that reading the book was like going
through jungle underbrush. It took him about 150 pages
before he began to like the book.[15] "Maybe this is what
happened to some other readers," he added.

They did not feel the need or have the
persistence to go past their initial stylistic
turn-off to the heart of the argument.[16] Their
loss. For you have something important to
say and it is something that no one has said
in this documented way before. I

15 Obviously the manuscript had serious stylistic and organizational
problems. The Schwendingers got a short delay from the editor at
the publisher while more than 24 students came to their aid and
helped them reorganize and edit the manuscript. The revised draft
was sent to the publisher.

16 The founders actively selected preexisting ideas that seemed to
deal with contemporary events; and The Chair had to show why
these ideas were important. Unfortunately, it pedantically devoted
160 opening pages to a variety of precursors even though their
relevancy could not be really appreciated until the transitional
theories, bridging the corporate phase of liberalism with earlier
phases, were presented.

congratulate you on it and thank you for it.

While Coser and Harris had no doubt that the book did not merit tenure at a major university, Wallerstein disagreed:

> I cannot understand these doubts. I can only say that it would be a salutary thing for American sociology if large numbers of the tenured faculty at our various major departments had written as good and as important a book. In these days of political polarization in our departments, there is a facile use of pseudo-academic criticisms of the work of others we do not like. But a sober appraisal of your work, and a careful one, should, in my view, end in a very positive note. I hope, for all our sakes, that you will get this sober and careful appraisal.

Wallerstein gave Schwendinger permission to use the review as he saw fit, but it was not sent to Messinger. In the first place, by then it was obvious that the review would be discounted because the School did not solicit it. Furthermore, by the time Wallerstein's review had arrived, Schwendinger had been informed that the second set of reviewers would only consist of UCB faculty members, Philip Selznick—a virulent anti-Communist and chief architect of the Law School department that was to replace the Criminology School—and two others, Leo Lowenthal, a lesser member of the Frankfort School whose works have passed into obscurity, and Philip Nonet who hardly deserves mention. Selznick and Nonet were close to Messinger and Skolnick, and they had met secretly to establish a politically sanitized "Law and Society" program at the Law School. Moreover, Skolnick,

Diamond and Messinger not only refused to get reviewers from other universities—they also rejected Paul Takagi's suggestion to include Troy Duster, David Matza or Robert Blauner even though they, too, were members of the UCB sociology department.[17] Since the second review took place as the School was being closed, using Wallerstein's reply to fight for outside reviewers would have been as exhausting and useless—as Platt's fight for tenure had proved.[18]

Down but not forgotten, Schwendinger was dismissed on June 30, 1975. He sought employment everywhere, but the radical reputation of *The Chair*—and phone calls by respective employers to UCB—put him on a blacklist. He applied for a UCLA sociology department position where he had been a graduate student but the faculty was deadlocked around his candidacy for two years, during which time no one else was hired.[19] The sociology faculty and two Deans approved his application at Boston University but the archconservative President Silber turned him down. The faculty at the California State University, Northridge, also voted to hire him, but the Liberal Arts Dean refused. And so it went.

Julia bravely kept her family afloat with the aid of Sheriff Richard Hongisto, who hired her to head the resource program for the San Francisco women's prison. Then, she obtained employment as an Assistant Profes-

---

17 At this point, the book had been edited but Messinger insisted on using the original unedited manuscript and refused to use the edited copy for the review.

18 Schwendinger was informed that Bowker allowed the Horton review to be included in the first review but a year later he was told that it would not be included in the second review, because it was not solicited by the senior faculty.

19 Schwendinger finally withdrew his candidacy so the people who supported him could work out a compromise with the other side.

sor at the University of Nevada, Las Vegas. But after two semesters teaching criminal-justice courses, other faculty members told her that she would never get tenure at "Disco Tech," as it was fondly called. She had filed an affidavit proving that a colleague had been denied "due process" when the senior faculty cowardly refused to grant him tenure because a conservative Regent had attacked him for adopting the textbook, *The Iron Fist and the Velvet Glove.* [20]

Fortunately, Herman applied to SUNY, New Paltz. Its Dean of Liberal Arts—after phoning "West Coast friends" who said Schwendinger was an "exceptional scholar"—approved the sociology department's unanimous recommendation.

The Schwendingers landed on their feet. Their books and articles have received the *Tappan Award* from the Western Society of Criminology, the *Distinguished Scholar Award* from the Crime, Law and Deviance Section of the American Sociology Association, the *Outstanding Scholar Award* from the Society for the Study of Social Problems, a *Scholarship and Research Award* from the Women's Division of the American Society of Criminology, and the Major Achievement Award from the Critical Criminology Division of the American Society of Criminology.

Herman was awarded the title of *SUNY Faculty Exchange Scholar.* (This SUNY-wide Academic senate award provided Herman with honoraria and travel funds to share his work with people on other SUNY campus-

---

20 Lynn Osborn also filed an affidavit. She was a UNLV sociology faculty member who had also graduated from the UCB School of Criminology. This was not the only occasion where she showed her courage. The Schwendingers remember visiting her in jail during her student days after she was arrested at a demonstration.

es.) He also received the coveted SUNY *Excellence Award* "in recognition of sustained, outstanding performance and superior service to the State University and the State of New York."

In 2010, the Schwendingers were included in a work entitled *Fifty Key Thinkers in Criminology.* This work featured philosophers, legal scholars and social scientists who had written landmark works from the 18th century onward.[21]. None of the faculty who denied Schwendinger tenure were included in that volume.

---

21 *Fifty Key Thinkers in Criminology*. Edited by Keith Hayward, Shadd Maruna and Jayne Mooney. London & New York: Routledge. 2010. The Schwendingers are covered in pages 159—162.

11 | Round Up the Usual Suspects!

R ichard A. Myren, a member of the Wolfgang Committee and author of *Education in Criminal Justice*, observed: "Berkeley exhibits probably the widest range of attention to crime studies of any university in the United States today."[1]

However, from 1973 tenured faculty covered all bets. To placate university authorities, Diamond, Skolnick and Messinger swiftly validated the half-truths and outright lies justifying purging the radicals. Previously, for example, Messinger had eagerly supported the move to broaden the curriculum; however, after the Sindler Committee claimed that the School had abandoned its professional mission, he proposed keeping the School but narrowing the curriculum, confining it to the "administration of criminal justice."[2]

Skolnick's turn-about also made the Sindler Committee credible. In a confidential memo to the Chair of the

---

1 "ASUC Committee Cites Services of Crim.School, *Daily Californian*, Volume V, Number 136, Wednesday, April 10, 1974 p. 1.

2 Messinger's memos to Charles Dekker, Committee on Educational Policy, and Sanford Elberg, Dean, Graduate Division, on June 28, 1973 and on July 11, 1973.

Academic Senate Committee on Educational Policy,[3] he wrote,

> First, I agree with the committee's recommendation that the School of Criminology ought to be phased out, but I don't agree with certain parts of the analysis. I believe it would be possible and desirable to have a School of Criminology that would, precisely because of its high academic standards, make important contributions. ... It seems to me that historically the school has suffered from extremes: either the police and correctional training orientation of earlier generations, or the antithesis–the grandly systemic, Marxist orientation of a sizeable proportion of the current generation of faculty.[4]

> Second, as one of the faculty who counseled a broader orientation for the School in the direction of Law and Society, I support the general trend of the recommendation, but find its specifics to be both inadequate and inconsistent. ... The resources now allocated to the School of Criminology should be shifted into a department–say of legal concepts, organization and institutions.

---

3 Confidential memo to Professor Charles Dekker, Chairman of the Academic Senate Committee on Educational Policy, June 25, 1973.

4 Only two professors at the School considered themselves Marxists. Diamond, in an interview with a San Francisco Chronicle reporter about the School closing, also employed a similar rational.

Although Skolnick juggled his recommendations with finesse, his memo clearly favored the second alternative— a "law and society" department. Undoubtedly concerned about his own continued employment, he repeatedly stressed the necessity for equipping this department with a core faculty and adequate funds.[5]

Diamond added his own patronizing counsel to this well-timed enterprise. After the administration in the final months made him the School's "Acting Dean" to oversee the closing, he affirmed his place on the side of the angels and loudly expressed his disdain for the School's standards and curriculum. Suddenly, this famous forensic psychoanalyst—whose "expert testimony" at the Robert Kennedy assassination trial claimed that Sirhan Sirhan wasn't legally responsible because he was psychotic—issued a memo requiring every remaining graduate student who had not taken a course in law to take one at the Law School.[6] He then conducted a vendetta against Takagi and Platt after they declined to ratify his attempt to fail an African-American doctoral student in an oral exam. He accused them of abandoning their academic responsibilities. To humiliate them, he insisted on bringing faculty in from other departments to monitor oral examinations taken by their doctoral students.[7]

They refused to submit to Diamond's arrogant disregard of their academic prerogatives. Of course, Platt had

---

5 But it would not include the much maligned criminalistics program, which he recommended terminating.

6 This idiotic proposal was dropped when graduate students expressed their outrage over this last minute requirement.

7 Four doctoral students who were affected sent written objections to Diamond. Also, Takagi rightfully refused to serve on any oral exam governed by these new conditions.

been denied tenure and the School's closing meant that he could not maintain his position. But tenured faculty at Berkeley were not dismissed unless the administration could prove that they had committed a crime or a serious breach of ethical standards. Takagi had tenure and the administration could not dismiss him on these grounds. Nevertheless, his courageous defiance of Diamonds' demands jeopardized his prospects. Despite his tenured position, Takagi's continued employment at UCB was not assured if the School was closed.

Diamond gave lip service to Berkeley mores. He had previously announced that he would only accepted the responsibility of Acting Dean if the senior faculty was assured of continued employment. But student protests and legal actions taken against his sycophantic and unnecessary acquiescence to authority[8] resulted in his unwillingness to do anything to ensure employment for Takagi, a senior faculty member. After the School was closed, Takagi was not given a position with Skolnick and Messinger in the Law and Society program at the School of Law in Boalt Hall. Instead, he was added to the faculty at the School of Education where he was isolated and left "twisting in the wind."[9] He did not receive a single merit increase in salary and retired 10 years later without being promoted beyond the rank of Associate Professor which he had at the School of Criminology.

To discredit the UC administration's treatment of Tagaki, we should note that his family in 1942 had been forcibly interned in Manzanar—the first of 10 permanent "War Relocation Centers" where almost 120,000 Japanese and Japanese Americans were incarcerated un-

---

8 He was particularly outraged over a civil suit, initiated against him by the African American student whom he failed.

9 See, Takagi 1999, op. cit.

til 1945.[10] (Two-thirds of the individuals in these intern- ment camps were American citizens.) During their in- ternment, young men were allowed to leave the camps when they volunteered to serve in a renowned unit that fought in the European theatre during WWII.

During the post-war years, Takagi was employed by the Alameda County's Adult Probation Department. By early 1963, he was a parole officer in Los Angeles work- ing with drug users and dealers. Three years later, he transferred to San Quentin Prison, where he worked as a classification officer for the California Board of Correc- tions.

Simultaneously, Takagi enrolled in Berkeley and Stanford. He finally received a PhD and joined the School of Criminology because of his notable contribu- tions to statistical methods and parole for government correctional agencies.

On January 21, 1969, the Third World Strike at Berkeley began and the Asian component of the student groups involved in the strike asked Professor Takagi to be their sponsor. He also co-taught the first course on Asian American history at Berkeley in the winter quarter of 1969. Also, Takagi was the faculty sponsor of an "ex- perimental course," then called Asian Studies 100X. To- day, Asian-American studies programs exist at 140 universities.

Takagi also sided with the students and faculty at the School who opposed the Vietnam War. In addition, his article, "A Garrison State in a 'Democratic' Society," be- came recognized as the pioneering study about the de- gree to which police used force when dealing with

---

10 Takagi was born in the US. His family history is described in

African Americans.[11]

During the 1980s, Takagi and Tony Platt were jointly awarded the Paul Tappan Award for 1980–1981, and Paul was elected the chair of the criminology section of the American Sociological Association, 1986–1987. He also received the National Council on Crime and Delinquency's Gerhard Mueller Award, which honors outstanding contributions to criminology that brought a global perspective to U.S. justice policy and advance human rights. He was also honored by the Association for Asian American Studies

Upon Takagi's retirement, Rep. Ronald V. Dellums honored him on the floor of the House of Representatives. Dellums had come to know him and his work over a period of two decades and "counted on his knowledge, his training, his wisdom, and his ability to articulate the critical issues and problems about the justice and penal system in the United States."

During these years Takagi helped edit *Crime and Social Justice*[12] and continued to contribute writings on criminal justice. While Carter was president, Tagaki was a consultant for federal agencies, evaluating criminal-justice proposals especially concerned with racial discrimination. He worked with the Justice Department on police use of deadly force and was invited to speak at annual meetings of black police officers' organizations. He was sought as a consultant by cities such as Berkeley and Portland on police chief selection, and gave talks at mandated cultural sensitivity workshops—where 46 judges, for instance, including the Alaska Supreme

---

11 See *Crime and Social Justice*, 1974 pp. 27–32.

12 The name of the journal was changed to *Social Justice*: *A Journal of Crime, Conflict and World Order.*

Court justices, were informed about the relations between racial discrimination and the criminal justice system. Other programs in which Takagi participated
included multi-cultural training of public-school teachers from the western United States and The National
Council on Crime & Delinquency's training program of
senior probation officers across the country.

Takagi's ill treatment when the School was closed
speaks volumes about the racist hypocrisy behind Bowker and Sindler's claims that the School was being abolished because it had lost its professional mission. Takagi
served at the School as the preeminent example of professionally dedicated faculty. No one—including Diamond, Messinger and Skolnick—came close.
Nevertheless, he was no longer able to teach graduate
courses in criminology. Platt, too, never taught graduate
criminology students again. Neither did Krisberg nor
Schwendinger.

A POST MORTEM TO END ALL POST MORTEMS

Caleb Foote, who shared an appointment at the School
of Law and the School of Criminology, walked lock-step
behind Diamond, Messinger and Skolnick. Frank Morn,
resorting to hyperbole, reported that Foote "had vivid
recollections of Dean Lohman's frenzied attempts to
maintain a balance between professional and academic
goals." To support professional training, Lohman, according to Foote,[13] admitted large numbers of "professional" teachers and "professionals as graduate students,
whose intellectual mediocrity and narrow vision hung
like a deadly pall over the school's intellectual climate."

---

13 Frank Morn, *Academic Politics and the History of Criminal
Justice Education*. Westport, Connecticut: Greenwood Press 1995
p. 105.

Morn added,

> Regarding the scholarship of the School of
> Criminology and the field, Foote believed
> that Lohman had overloaded the place with
> ill-conceived 'evaluative' or agency-action
> 'research projects' for which he had to hire
> staff of sufficiently limited vision to be
> willing to devote themselves to such trivia.
> As these researchers tended to drift into the
> teaching program whenever a course
> vacancy needed to be filled, the level of the
> faculty tended towards the same mediocrity
> that characterized the graduate student body.
> This, in turn, inhibited Lohman's efforts to
> recruit and retain able scholars.[14]

But Morn's report and Foote's so-called "recollections"
were wildly inaccurate. Foote surely would exclude his
friends, Messinger, Skolnick, Diamond and his Law
School colleagues who taught at the School, from his list
of "mediocre" "agency-action" researchers even though
they primarily dealt with legislative, juridical, correctional and police agencies. Yet, if the truth were told, the
"radicals" never engaged in "mediocre," "agency-
action" research. Platt had written an acclaimed *historical work* on the juvenile court and, before joining the
faculty, worked with Norval Morris at the University of
Chicago. Lohman had sponsored the Schwendingers' research project but that project was entirely based on
their causal theory.[15] Although it could prove useful for

---

14 Ibid.

15 Lohman was the principle investigator and Schwendinger the
Co-Principal because it was felt that the project, which was
devoted to Schwendinger's delinquency theory, would be funded
if the Dean had ultimate fiscal responsibility. As indicated,

"agency- action" research it tried to uncover the nature and parameters of delinquent subcultures. Finally, only a bonehead would use the word "mediocre" to label Takagi's or Krisberg's scholarship. Takagi was active in agency evaluation and training, but he also produced pioneering works on police killings of African Americans and the historical development of correctional institutions.[16] Krisberg, on his part, never was employed in "agency-action" research conducted at the School itself. He joined the faculty after graduating from the University of Pennsylvania, and his interests ran the gamut of criminological concerns even though they converged on delinquency prevention and control. Krisberg in 1976 published one of the finest historical accounts of the juvenile-justice system.[17] After the School closed, he became a research director and then President of NCCD, the foremost organization in the field of juvenile justice.

What about the veracity of Foote's arrogant reference to the students? Overwhelmingly, the so-called "mediocre" and "intellectually narrow" students became academics and directors of research institutes.[18] Their scholarly contributions to criminology can then and now be compared favorably with those from any graduate

---

Schwendinger, after all, was still a graduate student and preparing for his oral examinations when the NIH reviewed his proposal.

16 Paul Takagi, "A Garrison State in a 'Democratic Society.'" *Crime and Social Justice* 1 (Spring-Summer) 1974 pp. 27–33; and "The Walnut Street Jail: A Penal Reform to Centralize the Powers of the State," *Federal Probation* 39 (December) 1975 pp. 18–26.

17 Barry Krisberg, "Children of Ishmael." In (Eds. Barry Krisberg and James Aust) *Children of Ishmael*. Palo Alto: Mayfield Co., 1978.

18 In the 1967 to 1972 period alone, the number of post-graduates assuming academic posts (professorships) accounted for about 80 per cent of the graduate student population.

program in the country. They certainly were superior to Foote's law school students who were being trained to be legal practitioners rather than scholars. When the Sindler report was issued, about 80 percent of the students in the doctoral program had obtained jobs in universities and research institutes. Most of them are still employed today as professors, chairpersons and deans. One of the foremost criminal-justice research institutes in the United States, the Michael Hindelang Institute, is named after a student in the program at that time.[19]

The School's contribution also included graduates who became administrators in public institutions. Its graduates included the head of the Atlanta Police, director of the Georgia Juvenile Justice system, Chief of Police for Charleston (North Carolina), a General in the United States Army, Chief of Detroit police and the Sheriff of San Francisco County. One of the most famous United States prison reformers of the last century, Tom Murton, was a graduate of the School. As Superintendent of the Arkansas Correctional system, he courageously instituted democratic reforms, exposed administrative corruption and the assassination of prisoners by trustees, committed at the behest of the guards. Robert Redford dramatized him and his work in the Hollywood film, *Brubaker*.

The final reviewers, the Dekker Committee, also took the low road and its majority, without seeming to cave-in to the administration, tacitly legitimated the purge by

---

19 We would like to express our appreciation of Garafalo's acceptance of Herman's article in a Hindelang Institute publication on the historical origin's of the privatization of prison reform. He had received funds that supported his study but the government agency that provided these funds refused to publish it.

recommending replacement of the School with a "law, society and criminal justice" program in the School of Law. Their recommendation, however, was suspect because most of the Law faculty, including Caleb Foote, were "mediocre," "agency action" academics. The Law School was under fire from students who attacked its traditional law training and its conspicuous avoidance of affirmative-action policies. While two right-wing members of the Dekker Committee[20] demanded the immediate closure of the School of Criminology, Laura Nader, a professor of anthropology (and Ralph Nader's sister) dissented from the Committee's recommendation. On May 9, 1975, she co-signed a statement with two student members on the committee that said,

> The law schools of the state have been successful in training private lawyers for private concerns and the legal research done is most usually technical writing for lawyers, by lawyers. There has been glaring failure to research and write on subjects which interest the general citizen. Boalt Hall in particular has a reputation for being culture bound and traditional rather than innovative, and, is among the most professionally oriented of the leading law schools . . . we fail to see, when what we are dealing with is a social science endeavor, the necessity for 'complete administrative integration' with the law school—an institution with no commitment to social science research and teaching. . . . We question the competence of the law faculty

---

20 One of these members, Paul Seabury, had been condemned as a war criminal by anti-war tribunals set up by Berkeley students and residents.

> to train citizens to understand the operation
> of law in society, and at the same time to
> maintain goals of the profession as taught at
> the law school. That is, we raise doubts
> concerning the ability of the law school to
> accommodate philosophical perspectives in
> such a program.

In another minority report, student members of the Dekker committee, R. Harrison, A. Kolling and S. Smith, also expressed their objections: "after careful study, [they] concluded that two of these factors, the School's rejection of a professional mission and the absence of a viable academic field cannot be substantiated and that the faculty's disagreement on common goals (implicitly raised by memos written by Messinger and Skolnick) is not alone a reason for not continuing the School." They applauded "the services performed by and through the School for the community and the State; and the School's efforts in the area of affirmative action."[21]

Yet Morn's fairytale continued to reinforce lies about the School. Without citing sources, Morn said, "many considered criminology education as it existed in the School as a 'cheap' degree." Ignoring all the evidence to the contrary, he claimed, "there was remarkably little resistance or fanfare" to the closing of the School. He added, "In fact, many students later remembered with pride that they "had closed down the school."

---

21 R. Harrison, A. Kolling and S. Smith, *Minority Report on the Future of Instruction and Research in Criminology on the Berkeley Campus*. March 7, 1974, p. 3. (This report can be found in Report of the ASUC Academic Affairs Committee to Review the New Program in Law, Society, an Criminal Justice. Prepared by ASUC Office of Academic Affairs, Academic Review Unit, July 25, 1975.

Morn could have applauded a Hollywood production about the School's closing ending with lifeboats of sailors cheering as they witnessed their wounded ship go to the bottom."[22] Apparently, in Morn's scenario, the usual suspects among the faculty were mediocrities and the students, irresponsible sea-faring lunatics.

AS THE SHIP BEGAN TO SINK

Bowker and Sindler had difficulty scuttling the School; they couldn't make it sink fast enough with radical students supposedly cheering as it flipped stern upward Titanic-style and plunged to the bottom of the sea. At one point, in fact, Diamond, Kadish, Selznick, Skolnick and Messinger—who were busily reinventing a strategy used in 1961 to save the School when Lohman became Dean —distracted them. Kadish and his *compadres* now tried to prevent the School from being closed by recommending Norval Morris, from the University of Chicago Law School, to be the Dean of Criminology at Berkeley. This move, they felt, would placate Bowker because Morris was an eminent professor of law who could be counted on to administer a School swept clean of its radicals. However, too many students read Morris' *Honest Politician's Guide to Crime Control*,[23] and no amount of damage control could stop them from politely expressing their candid opinions when he visited the campus. Morris declined the offer to become Dean.

Unable to enter a familiar harbor because of stormy political weather, Diamond, Skolnick, Messinger and others reversed course, sailed to a cove where they met secretly with Philip Selznick and other members of the

22 Morn, op. cit., p. 113

23 Norval Morris, *Honest Politician's Guide to Crime Control*. Chicago: University of Chicago Press, 1970.

Law and Society Center.[24] Hoisting Boalt Hall's colors, they micromanaged the close of the School while formulating a plan for a Law School department for the study of "law and society." When their planning was completed, administrative demagogues invited a politically diverse group of faculty to meet and formally legitimate the plan. This duplicitous process secured Messinger's and Skolnick's posts at Berkeley, although the new "department of law and society" never gained the worldwide prestige and legendary status the School of Criminology had achieved.

Unlike the motley collection of ship's officers, the mutineers among the students and faculty continued to defend the School. Letters seeking support were sent to professionals in the United States and abroad.[25] All sorts of communications, memos, letters, petitions and handbills were sent to Bowker from Academic Senate committees, UCB faculty and students at large, including people who worked as criminal-justice administrators and specialists who said that the School had played a vitally important role raising issues that needed to be confronted by their agencies. At one point, Bowker reported that he had received from 50 to 60 letters about the School. And even though the administration decided that the School would be closed, the radical students fought them every step of the way.

Early in 1973, criminology students, accurately interpreting the Sindler report as a political purge, formed the

---

24 Reportedly, Selznick had once led a Trotskyite sect called the "Schachtmanites" but he had made a 180 degree turn and become a virulent anti-communist.

25 Support from 31 academics and researchers in England, for instance, urged Bowker to retain the School "as it was presently constituted," thereby retaining the radical faculty and courses.

Committee to Save the Criminology School (CSCS) to organize mass student support. Petitions, rallies, marches, demonstrations, letters to regents, administrators, faculty and newspapers followed. San Francisco Sheriff Richard Hongisto addressed a Sproul Plaza rally that spring followed by a march to California Hall, entering it with a list of demands. Two students were arrested and then released after the demonstrators agreed to leave the building. The students wanted reinstatement of undergraduate and graduate admissions to the school,[26] more resources for the school and an insured place for radical criminology. A campus-wide impeachment convocation at the Greek Theater was held in support of the School. Statements supporting the School arrived from the newly formed Berkeley Police Review Commission, Bay Area Women Against Rape, and criminologists in England, France, Italy, Netherlands and Norway. A petition with 3599 signatures supporting the school was submitted to Bowker by November.

Bowker, up to that time, had depended on the dilatory tactics learned at CUNY. Now, however, he rivaled the show, *Best Little Whorehouse in Texas,* by promising students that the university would satisfy their *every* desire. He said a much larger multidisciplinary interdepartmental program would replace the School. He gave them the same line he had given students who were trying to establish an ethnic-studies program and black studies school.

A million words justifying or opposing the School's closing were eventually produced by university authorities, the Sindler Committee, Academic Senate, Dekker Committee, Committee on Educational Policy, Graduate

---

26 The administration had terminated admission of undergraduate majors and graduate students.

Council, Criminology faculty, Student Association Committees, criminology students, Local 1474, student anti-war and civil-rights movements and the mass media. The central point to keep in mind, however, is that Bowker and the counter-reformist alliance never appraised the School in good faith. Their tactical vacillations were prompted by opposition from faculty at large, student demonstrations, and concern with the appearance of "due process" and moral legitimacy. They delayed announcing the decision to finally sink the School until the very end of the Spring 1974 semester—just before students were to return home.

During the previous year, the NLF, North Vietnam and the U.S. government signed a cease-fire agreement in January. By March 1973, the last U.S. troops left Vietnam and most of the remaining U.S. prisoners of war were released. U.S. bombing of Laos and Cambodia ended in August. In the following spring, Congress denied Nixon's request for additional funds to aid Saigon.[27]

Although several thousand students had turned out repeatedly to defend the School, the numbers dropped off in 1974. Just before the closing of the School was announced, about a thousand protested the plan to close the School on May 31. When asked about this final protest, Vice Chancellor Mark N. Christensen, remarked, "As I sit here and the students march around and I think about those poor bastards who were here a few years ago, I realize there is one big difference now. There's no unpopular war on now."[28]

---

27 On April 1975, Saigon was captured and the last U.S. personnel fled in a helicopter from the U.S. embassy compound.

28 Christiansen is quoted in William Trombly, "UC Student Protests: Peaceful Return to '64." *Los Angeles Times*, Monday, June 3, 1974, pp. 3, 29.

The battle for the School was lost but on the way we "poor bastards" had joined forces with others in the struggles for affirmative action, to defend women who were victims of violence, to bring the crime of rape out of the closet, to create a new criminology, to support prison reforms, and to fight police brutality. Also, we opposed a war in which more than 58,000 American troops were killed, over 153,000 were wounded and over three million Vietnamese were slaughtered. *To our everlasting credit, we joined with millions of people to help end the killing in Vietnam.* We helped end the war that McNamara called a "mistake" after the slaughter had occurred.

Sometimes we dream about those days, idealizing the people who fought for a School whose program we had helped to create. And we visualize our old colleagues and students encamped overnight in a valley surrounded by craggy California hills, singing, dancing and talking the hours away before sleep revived them for the struggle the next day. They conducted themselves honorably while the jackals howled in the hills.

§

Now introducing...

Thought | Crimes

The twenty-first century is an age of crime—state crime, corporate crime, crimes against humanity, crimes against nature. Elite crime. It is becoming increasingly clear that capitalism itself is a criminal system and the liberal democratic state a racket. In the current period of political repression, economic austerity, ecological destruction, criminalization of dissent, and mass resistance to these, the need for radical criminology is pressing. Radical criminology offers important insights into the composition of contemporary social struggles—and state maneuvers within those struggles. Radical criminology challenges openly practices of surveillance, detention, punishment and situates these within relations of exploitation and oppression that are foundational to capitalist society.

Notably, radical ("to the roots") criminological analysis is emerging from the movements as much as, even more than, from the academy. Indeed much of the most incisive thinking and writing in criminology is coming from movement organizers rather than academics. Fully open access, and an imprint of **punctum books**, the press is a project of the **Critical Criminology Working Group** at Kwantlen Polytechnic University. **Thought | Crimes** aims to bring together the most exciting and insightful new radical writings in criminology.

submissions * catalog * downloads / print:

www.thoughtcrimespress.org